IRON
BRIDGE TO
CRYSTAL PALACE

IMPACT AND IMAGES OF
THE INDUSTRIAL
REVOLUTION

A trade token issued in 1792,
showing the Iron Bridge at
Coalbrookdale (such tokens are
among the most interesting
illustrations of aspects of early
industrialization).

ASA BRIGGS

IRON BRIDGE
TO
CRYSTAL
PALACE

IMPACT AND IMAGES OF THE INDUSTRIAL REVOLUTION

*with 238 illustrations,
20 in color*

THAMES AND HUDSON

IN COLLABORATION WITH

THE IRONBRIDGE GORGE MUSEUM TRUST

Acknowledgments

The publishers wish to thank the Ironbridge Gorge Museum Trust for help and advice in the preparation of this book, and especially Mr David de Haan, Curator of the Elton Collection, for selecting items in the collection for use as illustrations and for supplying numerous photographs. Sources of illustrations other than those from the Elton Collection are: Arts Council of Great Britain *118*; Courtauld Institute, London (Col. Peter Arkwright Collection) *page 106 (top)*; Deutsches Museum, Munich *58*; Jorge Lewinski *pl. XX*; National Maritime Museum, Greenwich *80*; National Museum of Wales *pl. IV*; J. M. Oakes Collection *36*; Rhode Island Historical Society *49*; Royal Holloway College *p. 14*; Georg Schäfer Collection, Schweinfurt *75*; Smithsonian Institution, Washington, D.C. *98*; Science Museum, London *13, 60, 61, 63*; Sotheby's *76*; Tate Gallery *p. 15*; Thames and Hudson Ltd archives *pls III, V–IX, XI, XV–XVIII; 2, 6, 8, 10, 11, 21, 23, 25, 27, 39, 41, 45, 50, 51, 52, 56, 66, 70, 77, 78, 81, 82, 83, 88, 89, 90, 96, 101, 111, 113, 114, 123, 124, 130, 133, 135, 139, 141, 148, 149, 150, 151, 152, 153, 155, 156, 168, 179, 180, 186, 187, 188, 189, 190; pages 5, 37, 61, 82, 83*; Victoria and Albert Museum, London *97, 164, p. 175*; Walker Art Gallery, Liverpool *128*; Wedgwood Ltd *page 113 (bottom)*.

Library of Congress Catalog card number 79–63877

Printed in Great Britain by
Jarrold and Sons Ltd, Norwich

Contents

Title-page motif from *Le Génie
Industriel*, Paris 1851.

1 Nineteenth-century industrial progress and the
economic prosperity associated with the increasing use
of steam-power in Britain are here symbolized by the
passenger train with its enclosed carriages and by the
substantial station buildings (serving a different line)
in the background; by contrast, the abandoned and
decaying remains of a Midlands stage-coach hark back
to a past era. Chromolithograph by Henry Alken, *c.*
1841–5.

1 Prologue

THE TASK of erecting the ironwork of the first cast-iron bridge in the world was begun in July 1779. The bridge spanned the River Severn in Shropshire, one of England's most beautiful counties, but already for decades a scene of great industry. 'The neighbourhood is uncommonly full of manufactures', the great traveller Arthur Young observed three years before the bridge was completed. The decision to build it had already been taken, however, when Young singled out the 'potteries, pipe makers, colliers and iron works' in the district. Almost twenty years earlier, a local ironmaster had declared in a prospectus that 'there are perhaps few places where rural prospects and scenes of hurry and Business are so happily united as at Coalbrookdale'.

The very name 'Coalbrookdale' spoke for itself, and the ironwork of the new bridge was erected in three months 'without any accident to the work or workmen or the least obstruction to the navigation of the river'. The cast-iron members were manufactured at Abraham Darby III's ironworks at Coalbrookdale, the same works where (seventy years before) Abraham Darby I had for the first time in history smelted iron with coke instead of with charcoal. The Coalbrookdale works were the only ones in the world capable in the 1770s of producing cast-iron arches or ribs of huge dimensions. Even so, for this particular project the existing works had to be extended: the Old Furnace, for example, had to be enlarged and remodelled to a new design.

From the start the Iron Bridge fascinated contemporaries. It figured prominently in pictures as well as in poems and on tokens and tankards, even on the ash-holes of kitchen grates. 'It must be the admiration as it is one of the wonders of the world', wrote Viscount Torrington in his famous diary in 1784. The fact that the bridge was made of iron, the master material of the early industrial revolution, pointed to the future as much as it stirred visitors in the late-eighteenth century. Torrington noted that Coalbrookdale 'carts' were made out of iron and 'even the ruts of the road are shod with iron'. Sigfried Giedion in *Space, Time and Architecture* (1941) compared the bridge with the Church of the Fourteen Saints in Würzburg, finished in 1772. The church stood at the end of a tradition: the bridge opened 'a path for developments'. Iron could be used for buildings as well as for machines – and for much else besides. In the churchyard at Coalbrookdale it was even used in place of traditional tombstones, and John Wilkinson, enthusiastic pioneer and publicist of iron, who was directly associated with Abraham Darby III in the bridge-building enterprise, envisaged iron ships and desired to be buried in an iron coffin.

The single arch of the Iron Bridge had a span of just over 100 ft, and the rise of 45 ft consisted of five huge cast-iron ribs. The weight of iron in the whole interlocking structure was stated precisely and proudly as 378 tons 10 cwt. The structure looked durable as well as impressive. Soon after it was opened, Charles Dibdin, song-writer and dramatist, said of it that 'though it seems like network wrought in iron, it will apparently be

II, III
Frontispiece

uninjured for ages'. An American visitor, the Quaker Joshua Gilpin – the Darbys were Quakers, too – was rather more critical about its forms, as Giedion was to be. 'The Iron Bridge has a beautiful appearance on both sides – [and] has proved very strong – but is not built with Mathematical truth as the inner arch or rib in the main support of the two parallel ones . . . [is] no addition of its strength but much to the weight.'

The bridge was often repaired, but it survived and survives. It remained a toll bridge, indeed, until 1950, when it was handed over to the Shropshire (now Salop) County Council. It is now one of the great attractions of an English 'New Town', Telford, named after Thomas Telford, the outstanding engineer. New Towns, deliberately planned, are twentieth-century British enterprises, but by the mid-nineteenth century Shropshire, one of the cradles of the industrial revolution, was no longer a leading industrial county. It is the task of Telford New Town's Development Corporation, unique among such Corporations in having such a rich industrial heritage to safeguard, to ensure future economic and social developments in the locality.

'Improvement' is now as much the order of the day as it was in 1779. Meanwhile, the Ironbridge Gorge Museum Trust, founded in 1968, supported by the Corporation, has created, on a 42-acre site, an open-air museum concerned with industrial processes and products. In 1970 the Trust took out a long lease of the Darby Furnace site and has subsequently restored tracks, warehouses and cottages. Old industries are being revived with much of the same sense of 'hurry and Business' which had impressed Arthur Young.

The choice of the name 'Telford' for the New Town was appropriate, for Telford, born in 1757 – he was a Scotsman, like so many other leading figures in the industrial revolution – began his career in Shropshire. In 1796, he built the second iron bridge across the Severn, two miles away from the first, near Buildwas Abbey. The Menai Straits Suspension Bridge, completed in 1826, was one of his greatest triumphs. Another was the Caledonian Canal, 1822, 'one of the brightest examples of what the skill and perseverance of our engineers can accomplish', but not a commercial success. In 1820 Telford had become the first President of the Institution of Civil Engineers, founded two years earlier; and by the time he died in 1834 the railway age had begun.

'We who lived before railways and survive out of the ancient world are like Father Noah and his family out of the Ark', Thackeray wrote. Yet Telford spanned the divides. He had been offered the appointment of Engineer to the Liverpool and Manchester Railway in 1825, the year of the opening of the famous Stockton to Darlington line, four years before the victory of George Stephenson's *Rocket* in the Rainhill speed trials, in competition with four other locomotives. It was a Scots newspaper which said of this victory that it 'established principles which will give a greater impulse to civilization than it has ever received from any single cause since the Press first opened the gates of knowledge to the human species at large.'

Words never quite do justice to things, and this volume will be concerned with images as well as with words. Both, indeed, have to be considered together and in relation to each other. It begins with the origins and early development of industry in Britain, pointing to other centres besides Coalbrookdale and Ironbridge, and ends, as far as Britain is concerned, with the Great Exhibition of 1851, when a huge variety of things made in Coalbrookdale were on display. Significantly, the cast-iron gates at one entrance to the Exhibition were made at Coalbrookdale, a link between eighteenth and nineteenth centuries. Significantly, too, one of the features of the Exhibition was an unmistakably nineteenth-century artefact, the great ornamental rustic Coalbrookdale dome, 20 ft across and 30 ft high, which was described by the *Illustrated London News* as 'one of the most pretentious works in the building'.

To celebrate the bicentenary of the Iron Bridge, the Royal Academy Exhibition in 1979 provides a link between the eighteenth and twentieth centuries. The Royal Academy of the eighteenth century (it was founded in 1768) had little to do with industry. This task was left to the Society for the Encouragement of Arts, Manufactures and Commerce, which was set up in 1754, and it was this body which presented Abraham Darby III with its Gold Medal in 1788 and which, in addition to awarding medals, sponsored many exhibitions. It was this Society which took the initiative during the 1840s to launch an 'Exhibition of the Works of Industry of All Nations', the idea which came to magnificent fruition in the Crystal Palace in 1851.

The forerunner to the Royal Academy Exhibition in 1979 is a Smithsonian Institution exhibition in Washington, charting transatlantic and American industrial themes, and revealing the same logic of development. Coalbrookdale was one of the cradles not only of the first British industrial revolution but of world industrialization. Foreign visitors in the eighteenth century themselves recognized this likely outcome. It was difficult to set bounds to industrialization, and it was Tom Paine (who was as interested in designing iron bridges as Darby, Wilkinson and Telford) who wrote to Thomas Jefferson in 1789 after a visit to Yorkshire to discuss his bridge-building schemes, 'I have been to see the Cotton Mills – the Potteries – the steel furnaces – Tin Plate manufacture – White lead manufacture. All these things might easily be carried on in America.'

The year 1789 was, of course, the year of France's political revolution, and the Americans had already won their struggle for independence from Britain. The conception of a British 'industrial revolution', now a very hackneyed term, emerged fresh within this context. It was very likely a Frenchman, Jérôme Adolphe Blanqui, who first used it in 1827: 'While the French Revolution carried out its experiments on a volcano, England tried out hers in the field of industry. The end of the eighteenth century was signalled by impressive discoveries destined to change the face of the world.' France had Danton and Robespierre. Britain had James Watt and Richard Arkwright. These two particular names were associated with the steam-engine and the burst of invention in the textiles industry. Coalbrookdale had little to do with the second of these, which inevitably figures prominently in this book but it had much to do with the steam-engine *before* James Watt. The Darbys began casting iron engine-cylinders in 1722, and fifty-four years later in the year of the American Declaration of Independence built a Newcomen engine which remained in use for a hundred years. Two Watt engines were built for domestic use in 1787 and 1789 from drawings supplied by Watt himself. Richard Trevithick, the locomotive-builder, was in Coalbrookdale in 1796 and in 1802, and William Reynolds, grandson of Abraham Darby II, contemplated 'a subterranean tram road from the banks of the Severn right into the heart of the iron districts'.

The railway did not reach Coalbrookdale until 1857, by which time (despite the wide range of Coalbrookdale iron products displayed at the Great Exhibition) the Ironbridge area lay outside the main centres of industrial production. The Shropshire Canal was declining also. And it, too, had had its golden age. The Hay Incline, a huge inclined plane built in the 1790s to link the Canal with the Coalport Basin and the River Severn, remained in active use for some sixty years; it was last used in 1894 and the rails were removed in 1910, but it has now been cleared and re-railed by the Ironbridge Gorge Museum Trust. It is almost as impressive a sight as the Iron Bridge itself, a witness, once lost, to the energy and the imagination of the industrial revolution.

Like the Great Exhibition of 1851 and the bicentenary exhibitions of the Iron Bridge, this volume will concentrate not on the statistics of the industrial revolution or on explanation and interpretation of it, but on its images and its impact. Whenever possible the language of the times will be employed, not the language of economists or sociologists describing and analyzing it in the very different twentieth century. Even this approach now has its own history. It is now more than thirty years since Francis D. Klingender wrote his *Art and the Industrial Revolution* (1947), which was itself a by-product of a silver jubilee exhibition of the Amalgamated Engineering Union, given the title of 'The Engineer in British Life'. Klingender's book remains an indispensable study, but it was written not only before economists had turned to the industrial revolution as a major preoccupation but before the term 'industrial archaeology' had been coined. The vistas of 1979 are very different from those of 1947.

There is a special link, however, between this volume and Klingender's. The first half-tone illustration in his book, a 1750 engraving of Prior Park near Bath (reproduced also in this volume) was taken from the Arthur Elton Collection of pictures, books and other materials relating to industrialization. In July 1978 the Secretary of State for Education and Science allocated the Elton Collection to Ironbridge to be vested in the care of the Telford Development Corporation and to be administered by the Ironbridge Gorge Museum Trust. Sir Arthur Elton was a lively and discriminating collector. He was also a pioneer of visual education through film as well as through paintings and engravings, and the bicentenary exhibitions would have been after his heart. Many of the illustrations in this volume – and none of them are chosen simply to be decorative – come from the Elton Collection. Some of them have never been reproduced before.

To catch the flavour of the early industrial revolution and to appreciate its momentum, four kinds of illustrations are necessary – first, maps, for the topography of the revolution is fundamental, maps revealing the geography and the underlying geology; second, engineering and scientific drawings, for these were essential not only to the making of machines but to civil engineering projects which transformed the environment; third, paintings and engravings and, when possible, visual records of artefacts, for these express a wide range of responses to scenes and things, romantic as well as utilitarian; and fourth, photographs. The coming of the

photograph, recently much studied, was a subject of special interest to
Elton, who collected among much other photographic evidence William
Henry Fox Talbot's calotypes of the Great Exhibition, one of which was
reproduced by Klingender.

These four kinds of illustrations all have a direct relevance to Ironbridge
and Coalbrookdale. John Rocque's Map of Shropshire (1752) is a good
starting-point for any study of economic and social development, and there
is a fascinating plan of Coalbrookdale produced a year later and
reproduced by Arthur Raistrick in his invaluable book *Dynasty of Iron
Founders: the Darbys and Coalbrookdale* (1953). Engineering and scientific
drawings figure there, too, the first a 1776 drawing of the Handley Wood
Engine (built near Chesterfield in Derbyshire), cast at Coalbrookdale.
There is also an illustration of the model of 'the Coalbrookdale Iron
Bridge' which was made for the Society for the Encouragement of Arts,
Manufactures and Commerce in 1788, when Darby won the Gold Medal.

The development of wood and copper-plate engraving made possible
the production both of beautiful maps and of engineering and scientific
drawings which were works of art in themselves and not just blueprints;
and such was the general interest in them at the time that maps could
attract subscribers and engineering and scientific drawings could appear
in periodicals like *The Gentleman's Magazine* and even in *The Annual Register*.
The Ordnance Survey was officially established in 1791, but it was not
until 1870, when Britain had moved far towards industrialization, that the
one-inch survey covered the whole country.

A number of industrial communities are very well and very beautifully
mapped after the first stages of industrialization were complete. In his *Local
History in England* (1972 ed.), W. G. Hoskins had mentioned, for example
the Halifax map of 1852, published in thirteen sheets. 'One could pore over
it,' he says, 'for hours at a time.' Halifax was associated with industry
before the industrial revolution, and the 1852 map shows all mills (by
type), collieries (including disused pits), dye works, iron foundries,
quarries (for all the contemporary emphasis on iron as master material,
stone was a key material in the advance of industrialization), and so on.
The street names included Labour Street, Health Street and Temperance
Street. Professor Hoskins refers also to the less hopeful 'Bleak Street' in the
pottery town of Burslem – 'the mind boggles if even the Victorian optimists
thought it was bleak' – and Professor M. W. Beresford has written a
fascinating account of the often ironical history of Prosperity Street in
industrial Leeds. The detail is rich and significant although general
panoramas of Leeds give the sense of the whole. So, too, do the great
Victorian panoramas (notably of London) which precede the advance of
photography. There, map and cityscape are at one.

Engineering and scientific drawings have their own history, as
Klingender has shown. The people shown in the earlier drawings tended to
disappear in the late eighteenth century as the machines themselves
became more utilitarian and sometimes, though not necessarily, more
sophisticated. Moreover, as the processes carried out by machines became
more complex, there are limits to what a single engineering or scientific
drawing or even a set of them could reveal. The steam-engine, which was
popularized in an extensive literature, was frequently illustrated in many
different forms: so, too, were the different textiles inventions. (Lewis Paul's
patent for a 'spinning engine' in 1758 had five attached drawings with a

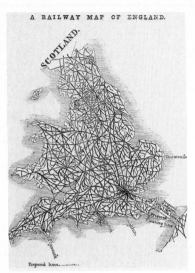

A *Punch* cartoon published in 1845 suggested the possible appearance of the map of England if the spread of railways were to continue unchecked.

long detailed text.) At one end of the scale were the Watt drawings (now part of the Boulton and Watt Collection in the Birmingham City Library), Sketch-book drawings and drawings for commercial purposes: at the other was Dionysius Lardner's *The Steam Engine Familiarly Explained and Illustrated with an Historical Sketch of its Invention and progressive Improvement*.

Telford prepared excellent drawings with the help of his draughtsman William Jones for his *Report on Mills* (1796–98); and, as Klingender pointed out, it is possible to trace the evolution of eighteenth-century styles towards 'the semi-abstract' in the six volumes of the *Designs of the late John Smeaton F.R.S. made on Various Occasions in the course of his Employment as a Civil Engineer from the Year 1754 to 1790*: these are preserved in the archives of the Royal Society. It is interesting to note that as the pressures of the industrial revolution intensified, the Royal Society lost touch with some of the most exciting advances in the provinces.

Other visual materials, which reflect a wide range of responses, also take a wide range of forms. Coloured prints and aquatints, the latter first produced in England during the 1770s, were the product of a partnership between engravers and colour-washers. During the early eighteenth century most of the tinted prints were line-engravings: by the end of the century, however, the techniques of etching, as expressed in aquatints, had become highly developed. During the nineteenth century many different kinds of colour reproduction were developed, so that it was possible by the time of the Great Exhibition to have 'traditional' engravings and lavish prints on paper (using George Baxter's patent process of 1835) alongside the photographs. Some watercolour painters, moreover, were using their medium in such a way that their pictures resembled oil paintings. Early railways, which figure prominently in the Elton Collection, are illustrated in many different *genres* – from draughtsman's sketches to gouache drawings, hand-coloured lithographs and watercolour paintings.

There are many interesting lithographs, and woodcuts were the staple of magazines like *Punch*, started in 1841, most of which prominently featured railways. 'Though England will never be in chains', exclaimed one *Punch* writer in 1845, 'she will pretty soon be in irons, as a glance at the numerous new Railway prospectuses will testify. It is boasted that the spread of railways will shorten the time and labour of travelling; but we shall soon be unable to go anywhere without crossing a line.' That was the lighter side, but railway accidents figured prominently in *Punch* also. 'A Railway is long, but life is short – and generally, the longer a railway, the shorter your life.'

Fear – along with horror – was often expressed in mid-Victorian cartoons, by which time excitement at the advance of technology was often darkened with doubt about social consequences. Some of the first eighteenth-century illustrations of industrial scenes had carried a sense of pride – pride in the machines and the ingenuity and the enterprise which they represented and pride in the heroism of the workers; and, of the great wheel constructed in 1820 at Styal in Cheshire it could be said that its 'slow and stately revolution seemed the very embodiment of power and dignity'. By the mid-nineteenth century, the pride had not been lost, but it was expressed more in words and in statistics than in pictures, and there was little talk of 'dignity'. There were few artists, indeed, who chose industrial themes. Even in the eighteenth century artists had been less concerned, perhaps, with dignity than with power, and many illustrations of industrial scenes had been characterized by delight in the 'picturesque' and later of the 'sublime'. Edmund Burke's *Philosophical Inquiry into the Origin of Our Ideas of the Sublime and the Beautiful* (1756: revised 1765) was published at the right time for people who had read it to appreciate Coalbrookdale. The first pictures of the dale did not bring out the sublime: many of the later ones did.

Verbal descriptions reveal the same shift in tastes. Thus, Arthur Young, writing after Burke, described Coalbrookdale as 'a very romantic spot; it is a winding glen between two immense hills which break into various forms, and all thickly covered with wood, forming the most beautiful sheets of hanging wood. Indeed, too beautiful to be much in union with that variety of horrors art has spread at the bottom; the noise of the forges, mills etc., with their vast machinery, the flames bursting from the furnaces with the burning of the coal and the smoke of the lime kilns, are altogether sublime, and would unite well with craggy and bare rocks, like St. Vincent's at Bristol.' The 'variety of horrors', themselves related to the sublime, almost in operatic form (cf. Weber's *Der Freischütz*), is well represented in the prints of George Robertson, later engraved, and, above all, Philip James de Loutherbourg's early nineteenth-century paintings. There were direct *III* links in the latter case both with music and with the theatre. Other industrial scenes painted by de Loutherbourg include *A View of a Blacklead Mine in Cumberland* (1787), not far from Wordsworth's beloved rural haunts of the Lake District, and *The Slate Mine* (1800). Not surprisingly, mines fascinated many artists, for they concerned both nature ('nature transformed') and industry. So, too, did canals, bridges and viaducts, which altered natural scenes, as, of course, did railways. The ambivalence about railways is well brought out by comparing scenes where the railway is an obvious intruder, destroying rural peace, and scenes where it fits naturally into the landscape or even 'improves' it.

It was not only minor artists who were attracted to such themes. Joseph Wright (1734–97) of Derby turned to science in his *Orrery*, *Air-pump* and *Alchymist*, and to industry in his *Glass Blowing House*, *Blast Furnace by Moonlight* and *Arkwright's Cotton Mill, Cromford*, the scene of his friend *36* Richard Arkwright's enterprise, near Matlock in Derbyshire. Canals inspired John Constable; so, too, did the opening of John Rennie's Waterloo Bridge in 1831. John Sell Cotman was fascinated by the great wheel at the head of the mineshaft at Coalbrookdale, and both he and David Cox painted Telford's great aqueduct at Chirk, near Llangollen. J.M.W. Turner, when industry had come to dominate much of the landscape, found Newcastle-on-Tyne something far more than a prospect: it was a world in itself, a world with its own atmosphere. The people return with the railways and the railway stations, not only for W.P. Frith, whose well-known *Paddington Station* was painted at the height of the Victorian period in 1862.

There was one remarkable artist, however, who would have scorned Frith's sense of life. John Martin used industrial elements in his brooding prints for an edition of Milton's *Paradise Lost* (1827) – coal-mines, tunnels, gasworks. He had spent the first seventeen years of his life in the Newcastle coalfield, and he actually submitted a 'plan for Working and Ventilating Coal Mines' to the Select Committee on Accidents in 1835. A year later he tried to launch a Metropolitan Sewage Manure Company. If his Hell and Heaven paintings borrowed from industry, engineers and industrialists in turn borrowed from him. Egyptian styles which he favoured were employed by I. K. Brunel in his plans for Clifton Suspension Bridge at Bristol (Telford's Gothic design was turned down) and for his railway viaduct at Hanwell. Brunel invited Martin to travel with him by railway in speed tests in 1841 from Southall to Slough, when a speed of 90 miles an hour is said to have been attained. This was in tune with the century, but *The Great Day of His Wrath*, the great apocalyptic work of 1851–2, inspired by the Black Country, was not. 'He could not imagine anything more terrible,' Martin's son wrote of him, 'even in the regions of everlasting punishment. All he had done, or attempted in ideal painting, fell far short, very far short of the fearful sublimity of effect when the Furnaces could be seen in full blaze in the depth of night.'

In general, nineteenth-century painters spurned the Black Country. In general, too, the industrial city, as it grew, was shunned rather than turned into a setting for interpretation. There were many charming scenes of eighteenth-century industrial towns, but in the nineteenth-century industrial towns there was usually too much feeling first of loss of nature and second of the social problems of the new city to keep the painter occupied there. Even in the eighteenth century the responses of poets were not dissimilar. Thus, Anna Seward, not however without her own ambivalences, could write in 1785 of 'violated Colebrook', 'grim Wolverhampton' and 'Sheffield smoke-involved'.

Paddington Station by
W. P. Frith, 1862.

Most local poets had similar reactions, even when they were proud of the progress of their localities and even, perhaps particularly, when they knew that in England 'Nature, was never very far away'. Thus, J. C. Prince, the Northern poet, described in 1841 how Sunday was the one day of escape not only from the relentless rhythms of industry but from the pressures of the city:

> Once more the ponderous engines are at rest,
> Where Manufacture's mighty structures rise;
> Once more the babe is pillowed at the breast,
> Watch'd by a weary mother's yearning eyes:
> Once more to purer air the artist flies,
> Loosed from a weekly prison's stern control,
> Perchance to look abroad on fields and skies,
> Nursing the germs of freedom in his soul . . .

Prince looked back to a time when

> As yet gigantic Commerce had not built
> Cities and towers, and palaces of pride –
> Those vast abodes of wretchedness and guilt
> Where Wealth and Indigence stand side by side;
> Man had not ventured o'er the waters wide.

The more industry developed its routines on the basis not only of new technology but of new forms of social organization (factories; railways; companies; cities) and new rhythms of work, the more backward-looking many artists and writers became. And again this process was true of great writers as well as lesser ones. Wordsworth had welcomed the early advances of science, writing enthusiastically in his 'An Evening Walk' (1788–9) of

> . . . those to whom the harmonious doors
> Of Science have unbarred celestial stores,
> To whom a burning energy has given
> That other eye which darts thro' earth and heaven.

Yet by 1802 he was less hopeful, and by 1814 readers of the eighth and ninth books of *The Excursion* (written a few years earlier) could learn how deeply disturbed he was about the spirit of his 'inventive Age' with 'its new

15

1 In order to demonstrate to
shareholders and public alike
that the Thames Tunnel project
(cf. *ill. 33*) first formulated by
his father was safe, the young
Isambard Kingdom Brunel
(who was in charge of the work)
held a banquet in 1827, with
fifty guests and over a hundred
miners seated inside the
partially completed tunnel. The
scene was recorded in an oil-
painting by an anonymous
artist.

and unforeseen creation'. Once again the rhythms seemed to him to be
wrong:

> And at the appointed hour a bell is heard,
> Of harsher import than the curfew-knell
> That spake the Norman Conqueror's stern behest –
> A local summons to unceasing toil!
> Disgorged are now the ministers of day;
> And as they issue from the illumined pile,
> A fresh band meets them, at the crowded door
> . . . Men, maidens, youths,
> Mother and little children, boys and girls
> Enter, and each the wonted task resumes
> Within this temple, where is offered up
> To gain, the master-idol of the realm,
> Perpetual sacrifice.

Wordsworth criticized both the new pattern of industrial relations and
the new environment:

> Where not a habitation stood before,
> Abodes of men irregularly massed
> Like trees in forests – spread through spacious tracts,
> O'er which the smokes of unremitting fires
> Hangs permanent.

This kind of double critique persisted throughout the century, often
carrying with it a critique of the machines and of the steam which sustained
them as well. As W.H. Henley wrote two years before 'the wonderful
century' ended:

> Here we but peak and dwindle:
> The clank of chain and crane,
> The whir of crank and spindle
> Bewilder heart and brain.

The looking backwards was most obvious, perhaps, in William Morris
(in his Introduction to *The Earthly Paradise*, 1868–70), although in time he
came to look forward to a socialist utopia:

> Forget six counties overhung with smoke,
> Forget the smarting steam and piston stroke,
> Forget the spreading of the hideous town;
> Think rather of the pack-horse on the down,
> And dream of London, small and white and clean,
> The clear Thames bordered by its gardens green.

So strong or persuasive are such voices that it is easy to forget two points
– first, that in the eighteenth century not all the nineteenth-century
schisms were already manifest and, second, that even in the nineteenth
century itself there were other voices. From the late eighteenth century the
voice of Erasmus Darwin, friend of Boulton and Watt (see below, p. 111)
and grandfather of Charles Darwin, has never been entirely stilled – even
by ridicule. Darwin was delighted by cotton-mills and optimistic about
steam. 'The further the artist recedes from nature, the greater the novelty
he is likely to produce; if he rises above nature, he produces the sublime.'

II, III Coalbrookdale, with its ironworks and later the
Iron Bridge built across the River Severn, attracted
many artists in the eighteenth and nineteenth
centuries. Among the best-known painters of industrial
subjects was Philip James de Loutherbourg, whose
Iron Works, Colebrook Dale was reproduced in 1805 as a
coloured aquatint (above, left) in *Picturesque Scenes of
England and Wales*. A coloured engraving (left), after
Michael Angelo Rooker's painting, shows the Iron

Bridge and its surroundings in 1782, two years after its
opening.

IV The Nant-y-Glo Iron Works, whose proprietor was
Richard Crawshay, were depicted in a watercolour
(now attributed to the artist George Robertson), *c.*
1788; the group of buildings on the left are probably
puddling furnaces and those on the right blast-
furnaces.

v–vii The era of steam-power inspired satirical fantasies such as this cartoon (left) by 'Shortshanks', *c.* 1830, as well as meticulously drawn documentary illustrations like John Emslie's coloured engraving (below) of a locomotive, published in James Reynolds's *Diagrams of the Steam Engine*, 1848. The sheer size of the Corliss steam-engine (opposite) – which operated all the working exhibits at the 1876 Centennial Exhibition held in Philadelphia – gives some idea of its 2,500 horse-power output.

LOCOMOTIVE ENGINE

VIII, IX The towering steam-hammer introduced by
James Nasmyth at his foundry near Manchester in
1832, as seen in a painting by its inventor; human
strength was here confined to manipulation, but
William Bell Scott's watercolour sketch for 'Iron and
Coal' – one of a series of eight murals painted on
canvas for Wallington Hall, Northumberland, in 1861
– reflected the Victorian idealization of physical
labour (the three figures wielding hammers were men
from Robert Stephenson's works at Newcastle).

Overleaf
x Henry Perlee Parker's
painting *Pitmen playing at Quoits,*
c. 1840, provides a faithful
rendering of miners' dress and
appearance while somewhat
sentimentalizing the harshness
of working conditions
experienced in nineteenth-
century collieries.

BE UNITED AND INDUSTRIOUS

AMALGAMATED SOCIETY OF ENGINEERS, MACHINISTS, MILLWRIGHTS, SMITHS, AND PATTERN MAKERS.

This is to Certify that _____ was admitted a Member of the _____ Branch, on the _____ day of _____ 18_ In Witness whereof we have subscribed our names and affixed the Society's Seal.

PRESIDENT.   SECRETARY.

XII Numerous artefacts decorated with illustrations of
places and events associated with industrialization
were made in many materials. This papier-mâché tray
bears a painting in oils of the opening of the Liverpool
and Manchester Railway in 1830, showing the
Moorish Arch at Edge Hill, Liverpool.

xv, xvi Every aspect of the Great Exhibition was
depicted and documented in great detail by many
illustrators. Part of the United States section,
surmounted by the symbolic eagle, is shown opposite.
The closing ceremony on 15 October 1851 (above)
was performed by Prince Albert and the
Commissioners seated on a dais and surrounded by
thousands of spectators.

XVII, XVIII The building of railways revolutionized travel in all parts of the world. A coloured woodblock print dating from *c.* 1880 (left) shows a simple station scene in Japan, while in America the Hornellsville Station and sidings on the Erie Railway – seen in a lithograph by Currier & Ives used to advertise that line in 1872 – convey some idea of the vast scale of the by then continental system (the east and west coasts were linked from 1869; cf. *ill. 77*).

XIX Industrialization introduced many new materials, often modestly at first. The young American petroleum industry in Pennsylvania – which figured as the title of a musical score published in New York – began in the 1850s as a source of fuel for lighting (kerosene) in place of whale oil. The crude oil was originally transported in barrels – and quantities are still measured in this way today.

To Miss H. Lilla Clarke.

AMERICAN PETROLEUM

This oil well threw pure oil 100 feet high.

This oil well is now flowing 355 Barrels daily.

LITH. OF HENRY C. ENO 37 PARK ROW NEW YORK.

The above Photographic View of the Tarr Farm Oil Creek P⁰ was kindly furnished by Wed W. Clarke & Co. 10 Pine Str N.Y.

Entered according to act of Congress A⁰ 1864, by W™ Hall, in the Clerk's Office of the District Court of the United States, for the Southern District of New York

POLKA, SCHOTTISCH, GALOP, WALTZ, MARCH.

BY

J. J. WATSON.

NEW YORK,

Published by W™ Hall & Son, 543 Broadway.

New Haven
Skinner & Sperry.

Buffalo,

Darwin's *Botanic Garden* (1789–91) is heavy with imagery as he sets out 'to inlist the imagination under the banner of science'. At Arkwright's Cromford

> . . . emerging Naiads cull
> From leathery pods the vegetable wool;
> With wiry teeth *revolving cards* release
> The tangled knots, and smooth the ravell'd fleece,
> Next moves the *iron hand* with fingers five,
> Combs the wide card, and forms the eternal line;
> Slow, with soft lips, the *whirling Can* acquires
> The tender skeins, and wraps in rising spires;
> With quicken'd pace *successive rollers* move,
> And these retain, and those extend the rove;
> Then fly the spoles, the rigid axles glow,
> And slowly circumvolves the labouring wheel below.

The vision is all of the future:

> Soon shall thy arm, UNCONQUER'D STEAM! afar
> Drag the slow barge, or drive the rapid car;
> Or on wide-waving wings expanded bear
> The flying-chariot through the fields of air.

Darwin wrote late in the eighteenth century, at the end of a decade of unprecedented economic expansion. 'Forges, slitting mills and other great works are created,' he noted in prosaic language free of allegory, 'where nature has furnished no running water, and future times may boast that this grand and useful [steam] engine was invented and perfected in our own country.' A generation earlier John Dyer, hailed by Wordsworth as 'Bard of the Fleece', had described in 1757 a Lewis Paul spinning-machine:

> . . . We next are shown
> A circular machine, of new design
> In conic shape: it draws and spins a thread
> Without the tedious toil of needless hands.
> A wheel, invisible, beneath the floor
> To every member of th' harmonious frame
> Gives necessary motion.

For Dyer, machines were making obsolete 'the tedious toil of needless hands', not displacing independent labour. And it was only the frame which was harmonious. The mill itself was a 'delightful mansion', and 'cheerful' were 'the labours of the loom'. The cities were not problem centres: they were 'all in motion':

> Th' increasing walls of busy Manchester,
> Sheffield and Birmingham, whose reddening fields
> Rise and enlarge their suburbs.

Even the work of children was good, as it had been to Daniel Defoe more than a generation earlier: it even had a pastoral quality.

> . . . The younger hands
> Play at the easy work of winding yarn
> On swiftly-circling engineer, and their notes
> Warble together as a choir of larks.

This was a period when 'industry' was not a sector of the economy, but a human quality, the mainspring of prosperity:

> . . . Industry
> Which dignifies the artist, lifts the swain,
> And the straw cottage to a palace turns,
> Over the work presides.

Dr Samuel Johnson complained that Dyer's interest in such themes pinned his poetry down: 'the wool comber and the poet appear to me such discordant natures, that an attempt to bring them together is to couple the serpent and the fowl'. Dyer was not alone, however, in choosing such themes. In similar mood, 'Commerce' had been saluted by John Dalton in his *Descriptive Poem Addressed to two Ladies, At Their Return from Viewing the Mines near Whitehaven* (1755), not the first poem to describe a mine, but possibly the first to describe a steam-engine:

> These are the glories of the Mine!
> Creative commerce, these are thine!

Whitehaven was then one of the leading ports in England. And from Birmingham, which was already and was to remain one of the leading industrial cities in the world, John Freeth wrote not long afterwards:

> Sons of *Commerce*, haste to pleasure
> For the joy belongs to you:
> May you live to reap the treasure
> That must happily ensue.
> Treasure from Staffordian plains
> Richer then Peruvian mines . . .
> All over the country shall gladness be shown,
> The Tradesman, Mechanic, and Cottager too,
> Shall all share the bounty that soon must ensue.

It is even more easy to divide poets into 'optimists' and 'pessimists' about industrialization than it is to divide economists and economic historians, a fashionable preoccupation among historians in recent years, for there is an obvious chronological divide in poetry after 1800. Thereafter, although the optimists do not disappear – the young Rudyard Kipling was one of them, and in the twentieth century Rupert Brooke could extol 'the keen unpassioned beauty of a great machine' – there was a revulsion.

It should be remembered, however, that the poets or would-be poets included engineers and scientists. James Clerk Maxwell enjoyed verse-writing at least as a pastime, and Telford himself wrote poems. Interestingly, they were pastoral poems set deep in the countryside far from the 'artificial joy' of towns:

> Deep 'mid the green sequester'd glens below,
> Where murmuring streams among the alders flow,
> Where flowery meadows down their margins spread,
> And the brown hamlet lifts its humble head.

'Escape' was the main urge, not the attempt to 'get inside' machines or to prophesy. By contrast, William Blake, who knew that second urge and whose poems are profoundly prophetic, was shocked by what he contemplated:

. . . All the arts of life they chang'd into the arts of death;
The hour glass contemn'd because its simple workmanship
Was as the workmanship of the plowman, & the water wheel
That raises water into cisterns broken & burn'd in fire
Because its workmanship was like the workmanship of the Shepherd:
And in their stead, intricate wheels invented, wheel without wheel,
To perplex youth in their outgoings, & to bind to labours
Of day & night the myriads of Eternity, that they might file
And polish brass & iron hour after hour, laborious workmanship,
Kept ignorant of the use: that they might spend the days of wisdom
In sorrowful drudgery, to obtain a scanty pittance of bread.

It is not surprising that critics have identified 'Marxist' themes in Blake, themes which were explicit in Morris.

Klingender wrote from a Marxist standpoint, too, beginning the first of his footnotes with a reference to Marx's analysis of the industrial revolution as a social process (*Das Kapital*, vol. I, 1867) and introducing his seventh chapter, 'New-Fangled Men', with a quotation from a revealing speech by Marx at an 1856 banquet in London. Marx extolled the progress of industrialization, but saw in it inevitable contradictions. 'On the one hand, there have started into life industrial and scientific forces, which no epoch of the former human history ever suspected. On the other hand, there exist symptoms of decay, far surpassing the horrors recorded of the latter times of the Roman Empire. In our days everything seems pregnant with its contrary; machinery gifted with the wonderful power of shortening and fructifying human behaviour we behold starving and over-working it. The newly fangled sources of wealth, "by some strange weird spell", are turned into sources of want. The victories of art seem bought by – loss of character. At the same pace that mankind masters nature, man seems to become enslaved to other men or to his own infamy. Even the pure light of science seems unable to shine but on the dark background of ignorance.'

Not surprisingly, there is a strong note of rhetoric here as there had been in the *Communist Manifesto* of nearly a decade earlier, which drew the sharpest possible contrasts while lyricizing the triumphs of industry based on steam-power. In his *Grundrisse*, only recently studied in this country, however, and in *Das Kapital*, well known to Klingender, Marx tried to explain what looked at first sight like the workings of 'some strange weird spell' (see below, p. 170). Others have attempted different explanations, though it remains difficult to dispense with the language of myth. Thus David S. Landes calls his study of 'technological change and industrial development in Western Europe from 1750 to the Present' *The Unbound Prometheus*. (Professor Peter Mathias, Chichele Professor of Economic History at Oxford, chose for his study of the British industrial revolution, however, the title *The First Industrial Nation*.)

The story of the poetry of industry from Blake and before to Morris and after is just as complex in its shades as the story of the statistics of the industrial revolution, and it has been well established since Klingender in *The Industrial Muse*, an anthology with admirable notes, edited by Jeremy Warburg (1958). More recently (1974) it has been supplemented by the study of Martha Vicinus, also called *The Industrial Muse*, which does not cover the same ground and which draws upon 'voices from below', 'literature as propaganda' and 'street ballads and broadsides: the foundations of a class culture'. The latter *genres* were often illustrated, usually with woodcuts. They could sometimes offer consolation rather than inspiration. Occasionally they could be fatalistic, as in John Grimshaw's 'Hand-Loom versus Power Loom':

> Come all you cotton-weavers, your looms you may pull down;
> You must get employ'd in factories, in country or in town,
> For our cotton-masters have found out a wonderful new scheme,
> These calico goods now wove by hand they're going to weave by steam.

The final stanza is even tougher:

> So, come all you cotton-weavers, you must rise up very soon,
> For you must work in factories from morning until noon;
> You mustn't walk in your garden for two or three hours a day,
> For you must stand at their command, and keep your shuttles at play.

All the same notes which were struck in poetry, including popular poetry, were struck, too, in late-eighteenth-century and nineteenth-century prose. The note of optimism continued to be heard, but it was countered by relentless criticism – from Southey to Carlyle, Ruskin to Morris, D. H. Lawrence to F. R. Leavis. Steam-power and railways were key themes here, too, and both could be treated symbolically as well as factually, as they were in Dickens. The verbal images of industry in Dickens were as powerful, indeed, as any pictorial images. *Dombey and Son* (1848), in particular, has many unforgettable railway images, and *Hard Times* (1854), influenced by Carlyle, presents a picture of 'Coketown' which was powerful enough to stir twentieth-century sociologists of cities, like Lewis Mumford. Indeed, Mumford took 'Coketown' as the generic name for all industrial cities, including those which followed in the English wake – Lille, Essen and Pittsburgh.

It is important to bear in mind that Dickens's verbal pictures are not photographs as they are sometimes taken to be. They were impressionistic on the surface and below the surface drawn from the crucible of Dickens's own unique experiences . . . city as prison; factory as discipline; the travesty of human relations when 'the cash nexus', as Carlyle called it, destroyed good will towards men. Other great nineteenth-century writers on industrialization, notably Ruskin, were drawing on their own unique experiences also. Ruskin's eye was not a camera. He began the second volume of *The Stones of Venice* on the day the Great Exhibition opened in Hyde Park, and he had no doubt about either his preferences or his priorities. 'To watch the corn grow, and the blossoms set; to draw hard breath over ploughshare or spade; to read, to think, to love, to hope, to pray. . . . The world's prosperity or adversity depends upon our knowing and teaching these few things; but upon iron, or glass, or electricity, or steam in no wise.' Britain had sold its soul to iron and steam.

The year 1851 was the year not only of the Exhibition, the 'romance' of which was spurned by Ruskin, but of the census which prompted G. M. Trevelyan to add to his statement that 'John Bull was ceasing to be a countryman and a farmer' the question, 'when once he was wholly urbanized or suburbanized, would he any longer be John Bull except in the cartoons of *Punch?*'. Yet so strong was the sense of break and so compelling the nostalgia that after the 1850s, as industrialization came to be taken for granted, there was a powerful bias against it, beginning in schools and universities and gaining strength in the adult population through poetry and pictures, articles and treatises. The Americans, whose industrial revolution came later (though its origins were traceable earlier, often in parallel with early nineteenth-century changes in England), seldom reacted in quite the same way. The geography and the social structures were different, and the élites, particularly from the late nineteenth century onwards, were minorities among minorities. Yet as Leo Marx has shown in *The Machine in the Garden* (1964), 'the whistle of the locomotive' could disturb rather than excite across the Atlantic also, and through different generations there have been several versions of American pastoralism. Nor are they dead. 'The soft veil of nostalgia that hangs over our urbanized landscape is largely a vestige of the once dominant image of an undefiled, green republic, a quiet land of forests, villages and farms dedicated to the pursuit of happiness.'

An illustration from Pugin's *Contrasts*, 1841, to show how the rebuilding of a medieval town and the introduction of industry might transform the general appearance of the place – and not for the better.

Some of the differences between the British and the American industrial experience are discussed in the Epilogue. But before insisting on later contrasts, it is necessary to trace earlier affinities. For Samuel Smiles, who was one of the most enthusiastic spokesmen of the new industrial system, 'everything in England' was 'young'. 'We are an old people, but a young nation', he wrote in his *Lives of the Engineers* (1861). 'Our trade is young, our engineering is young, and the civilization of what we call "the masses" has scarcely begun.' The people Smiles favoured, as Professor Thomas Parke Hughes wrote in the Introduction to his Massachusetts Institute of Technology edition of *The Lives* in 1966, were 'developing people' – the kind he described in his best-seller *Self-Help* (1959) – and the areas he was mainly interested in were 'developing areas'. There was an American flavour to all this, though Smiles was born in Scotland and spent some of the formative years of his life in the North of England. He quoted with approval in *The Lives* a letter from Telford written in 1800 in which the engineer generalized about the huge English area from the mouth of the Mersey at Liverpool to the mouth of the Severn at Bristol. 'This is an extensive district, abounding in coal, lime, iron and lead. Agriculture too is improving, and manufactures are advancing in rapid strides towards perfection. Think of such a mass of population, industrious, intelligent, and energetic, in continual exertion. In short, I do not believe that any part of the world, of like dimensions, ever exceeded Great Britain, as it now is, in regard to the production of wealth and the practice of the useful arts.'

A second example of 'Americanism' was a lively interest in the machines which were agents of 'improvement' and a pride in the hard-working qualities of the people. In the late eighteenth century 'wonders' were visible, and they could be greeted with awe:

> The time may come when nothing will succeed
> But what a previous Patent hath decreed;
> And we must open on some future day
> The door of Nature with a patent key.

These lines were written in 1776 when 'opening the door of Nature' seemed the most exciting task possible, the realization of Francis Bacon's vision in the seventeenth century. It was *after* 'the loss of the American colonies', as if by way of providential compensation, that 'discoveries and improvements' were thought to 'diffuse a glory over this country unattainable by conquest or dominion.' For the American 'Thomas Tollbooth', writing in 1799, Arkwright's 'invention of spinning cotton' and the inventions of Wedgwood and Watt more than made up for 'the losses of that disastrous war' which only came to an end in 1783. And delight in 'machinery' persisted through the railway age at least until the Great Exhibition of 1851. As Professor Eric Hobsbawm has written in his *Industry and Empire* (1968), 'Britain had certainly not lacked that acute, even irrational joy in technical progress as such, which we think of as characteristically American. One can hardly imagine the railways being developed, let alone built, in a country or by a business community which was not excited by their sheer technical novelty . . . for their business prospects were known to be relatively modest.'

The 'conquest of nature' was associated more with the discovery of steam-power than with machinery in general. When James Boswell visited Matthew Boulton's Soho Works in Birmingham in 1776, Boulton told him proudly that he sold 'what all the world desires, power'. For centuries the world had relied on animal power and wind and water. Now steam could transform not only Britain but the world. Dionysius Lardner called the steam-engine 'the exclusive offspring of British genius fostered and supported by British capital', but its benefits were deemed to be 'universal':

> Steam! – if the nations grow not old . . .
> Why dost not thou thy banner shake
> O'er sea-less, stream-less, lands, and make
> One nation of mankind.

These lines of Ebenezer Elliott, the Sheffield working-class poet, written in the early railway age, were part of a poem called 'Steam in the Desert'. There is a huge literature about 'the rise of steam' – including literature with a satirical edge and literature with a note of horror in it. But the hope carried by steam extended even to the desert.

It is interesting to note also that as steam made its way into English farms as well as English factories, the term 'horse power' survived the technical changes of the eighteenth and early-nineteenth centuries, just as it survived the late-nineteenth- and twentieth-century change from the coach to the motor car. Nor were wind- and water-power rendered completely obsolete by steam. It is perhaps equally interesting to note that Edmund Cartwright, the inventor of the power loom, actually experimented with the use of a bull to drive his loom.

There was a third example of 'Americanism'. It was not only the inventors or the businessmen who were singled out for their enterprise in the eighteenth century but the working men for their energy and industry. The French economist J. B. Say, who had worked in a cotton-spinning mill before becoming a mill-owner himself, maintained in 1826 that the 'England of today owes her immense wealth less to scholars . . . than to the remarkable ability of her entrepreneurs and to her workers for first-rate and prompt execution.' British workers (see Chapter III) were renowned in the 1840s for their work in railway building and contracting abroad as well as at home, and the French sociologist, Le Play, observed that he had found 'nowhere in Europe, except in England, workmen capable for an entire day, without any interval of rest, to undergo such a toilsome and exhausting labour as that performed by . . . Sheffield workmen.'

Hard work was one quality: skill was another. The first industrial revolution in the world did not take place in a backward country. It took place in a society where there were many skills, considerable experience of 'industry', and a thriving commerce with a strong outward-looking orientation. 'Cannot the industrial revolution be explained', R. M. Hartwell has asked, 'as the outcome of a process of balanced growth . . . the product of long-term and wide-spread change in England?'

The antecedent centuries cannot be ignored in any interpretation of the first industrial revolution which looked and still looks different in the light of what had come before from how it looks now. The uncle of the twentieth-century historian Arnold Toynbee, a historian of the same name and one of the first writers to popularize the concept in the nineteenth century (at a time when most historians ignored industrialization), claimed (1884) that the essence of the revolution was not the furnace or the steam-engine or even the textiles inventions but 'the substitution of competition for the mediaeval regulations which had previously controlled the production and distribution of wealth'. More recent writers have dwelt on the once-and-for-all shift from agriculture to 'industry', a slow shift, none the less, which took time to work out: indeed, industry and agriculture were closely integrated in the eighteenth century, not only through the use of natural resources (timber, stone, water and on to coal, iron and steam, not to speak of cotton and wool) or through industrial processes involving natural products (from brewing to spinning and weaving), but through complex interdependences (in banking, for instance, and through food supply). Some writers have looked to world interdependences and the development of triangular trade between Africa, America and Britain, a trade with a longer history than the early industrial revolution itself. Others have turned to the world of thought. 'An immense impulse was now given to science,' Sir John Herschel said of England after Francis Bacon, 'and it seemed as if the genius of mankind, long pent up, had at length rushed eagerly upon Nature, and commenced, with one accord, the great work of turning hitherto unbroken soil, and exposing the treasures so long concealed.'

There were practical anticipations, too, in such seventeenth-century activity as the improvement of river navigation or the draining of the Fens.

Thus, eight years after the death in 1677 of Cornelius Vermuyden, drainer of the Fens, the following lines were written:

> I sing Floods muzled and the Ocean tam'd
> Luxurious Rivers govern'd and reclam'd,
> Water with Banks confin'd as in a Gaol
> Till kinder Sluces let them go on Bail.
> Streams curb'd with Dammes like Bridles, taught t'obey
> And run as straight, as if they saw their way.

In the light of what came afterwards, the theme of the Epilogue to this volume, the British industrial revolution was merely the first of a series. The technology was dated and has been replaced by newer and far more sophisticated technology, the exploitation of resources was limited and primitive, the interdependences were severely restricted in their implications, and the ways of working and managing were crude and exploitative. Even the underlying 'thought' itself seemed crude and primitive, too, to chemists working in an age of synthetics, to physicists working in an age of nuclear power and to engineers working in an age of computerization. The perspectives are always changing. For a time the term 'second industrial revolution' was popular within a world context, covering changes both in techniques and in organization. Now, however, with the growing sense, at least in the United States and in some parts of Europe, that society is changing from an industrial society (with continuing industrial revolution) to a post-industrial society (with new social structures and with new attitudes to work and leisure) the whole experience of industrialization is being reviewed afresh.

Some of the changing images of industry have been reviewed in this chapter. No account of present perspectives would be complete, however, if it did not take account first of photography and second of 'industrial archaeology'. Old photographs, already mentioned, are indispensable sources, although there were fewer nineteenth-century photographs of industrial scenes and, above all, of industrial processes than of rural (or seaside) scenes and of family occasions. The Church was a more congenial subject than the Factory, the Beach more congenial than the Mine. In the later twentieth century however, every surviving relic of early industrialization has been photographed. *Ironbridge, Landscape of Industry* (1977) by Neil Cossons and Harry Sowden, includes a wide array of Sowden's photographs of Coalbrookdale as it is today, including photographs of houses and sites in the course of restoration. Among them is a photograph of the secret enclosure of the Quaker Burial Ground, where all the tombstones of the Darbys are kept except that of Abraham Darby I. The stones in the burial-ground have all been removed from their original positions and line the surrounding wall.

For England as a whole, Anthony Burton's *Remains of a Revolution* (1975) contains twenty-four pages of colour photographs and sixty-four pages of black and white photographs by Clive Coote, including one of Ironbridge and one of Telford's road bridge across the River Dee. They give impressive evidence of the extent and quality of England's 'industrial heritage', a heritage which is being increasingly treasured. Some of the pictures, none the less, are of dilapidated or abandoned industrial sites and buildings. Thus, in the chapter on the Potteries, one of the country's most distinctive industrial areas, there is a moving picture of 'the sad dereliction that was once Wedgwood's Etruria Works'.

'Industrial archaeology' was a term which came into use only during the 1950s; yet Sowden and Coote's photographs, considered independently, show how active a pursuit it has become in recent years. In 1955, writing in the *Amateur Historian*, Michael Rix anticipated a main plank in the argument of this volume: 'Great Britain as the birthplace of the industrial revolution is full of monuments left by this remarkable series of events. Any other country would have set up the machinery for the scheduling and preservation of these memorials that symbolise the movement which is changing the face of the globe, but we are so oblivious of our national heritage that, apart from a few museum pieces, the majority of these landmarks are neglected or unwittingly destroyed.' Rix went on to specify 'the steam engines and locomotives that made possible the provision of power, the first metal-framed buildings, cast-iron aqueducts and bridges, the pioneering attempts at railways, locks and canals', and, not least, workshops, mills and factories. Industrial archaeology he contemplated as 'a fascinating interlocking field of study, whole tracts of which are still virtually unexplored.'

Rix was wrong to argue that 'any other country' would have 'set up the machinery' or that Britain was exceptionally 'oblivious' to its national heritage. And his statement restricted the field of the subject too narrowly to the 'early industrial revolution', the period covered in this volume. He underestimated, too, perhaps, the love and care which 'industrial archaeology' would invoke when it widened its appeal far beyond existing circles of interested 'amateur historians'. Coalbrookdale and the town of Ironbridge provide excellent examples. The capital cost of the distinctive combination of preservation, recovery and development is inevitably high, but paid workers, 'Job Creation' scheme workers and volunteers have collaborated better in teams than most workers in modern factories, warehouses or hospitals. They have had a goal, and, above all, they have displayed the kind of enterprise that characterized the industrial revolution itself. Not least, they show sensitivity. They recognize that – in the words of Neil Cossons who, as Director of the Museum Trust, is deeply involved in the whole scheme – 'even the sense of decay, and the feeling that time has stood still, are ingredients which impart a particular quality to places like Ironbridge, Coalbrookdale and Jackfield'.

Michael Rix singled out Coalbrookdale in his 1955 article as 'the cradle' of early industrialization, and four years later Allied Ironfounders opened to the public the Darby Furnace site, carefully excavated and restored, together with a small museum of ironfounding to commemorate the 250th anniversary of the coke-smelting process. Thereafter, work at Ironbridge became increasingly influenced by public policy as well as by private enterprise, and the enthusiasm of amateur historians continued to provide inspiration and effort.

In 1959, the year of the opening of the Darby Furnace site and the museum, the Council for British Archaeology expressed the need for national concern in the often urgent tasks of industrial archaeology. Archaeologists had sometimes declared such interest in the Victorian past:

in 1878, for example, the *Transactions of the Cumberland and Westmorland Antiquarian and Archaeology Society* included a useful paper by Isaac Fletcher, 'The Archaeology of the West Cumberland Coal Trade'. Such articles – and this one was mentioned by Kenneth Hudson in his valuable introduction to the subject, *Industrial Archaeology* (1963) – represent 'the other side of the Victorians', since most Victorian archaeologists fled from the cities, and turned to a more remote past. The support of the Council for British Archaeology in 1959 was significant, and the appointment as Consultant of Rex Wailes, a retired engineer and past President of the Newcomen Society, was crucial. His task was to advise on the scope and nature of the problems of the classification and conservation of Britain's 'industrial monuments' so that decisions could be taken as to how far the then Ministry of Public Building and Works should be involved and as to whether existing legislative provision was adequate. Wailes was fully supported by the Ancient Monuments Board, a sign that the remote and the recent (or relatively recent) are not necessarily conflicting periods of interest. The distinguished archaeologist, Professor W.F. Grimes, was active at all stages.

The initial survey was not easy to carry out, and all the time fascinating old industrial buildings and sites were being destroyed. The pulling down of mill chimneys was symbolic. Once associated – in the literary imagination, at least – with 'dark Satanic mills', they now began to acquire a rarity value. Gasworks went, too. Yet the survey and its supporters had powerful forces on their side – a growing interest in the environment as a whole, and in the heritage. European Architectural Heritage Year (1975) was witness to this: so, too, was the subsequent formation of the Heritage Education Group, which carries the interest into schools and into deprived places where there is no conspicuous 'historical heritage'; developing urges on the part of individuals and groups to use old buildings for new purposes (brilliantly depicted in the United States in Barbaralee Diamonstein's *Buildings Reborn: New Uses, Old Places*, 1978); extended curiosity on the part of tourists, fostered by bodies like the English Tourist Board; the increasing fascination of small groups of enthusiasts for 'vintage machines' (the more twentieth-century railway networks were reduced, the more enthusiastic the railway enthusiasts became); the boom in labour history, leading to a bigger boom in 'history from below', itself exploiting the new techniques of oral and visual history and encouraging the growth of 'history workshops'; the parallel boom in local history and in urban history, subjects which lent themselves to co-operation between 'amateur' and professional historians; the rise of new universities, like Bath, where there were possibilities of new lines of academic action. The Centre for the Study of the History of Technology of Bath University, under the supervision of Dr Angus Buchanan, took over the task of compiling a National Register of Industrial Monuments.

When Wailes retired from his full-time post in 1971, to be succeeded by Keith Falconer, much had been accomplished, although it was clear how much still remained to be done. By then there was a government Department of the Environment, and its inspectorate was closely involved in industrial conservation. A further important change took place five years later when the existing Survey Panel, virtually a sub-committee of the Council for British Archaeology, was replaced by a smaller body, backed by corresponding members and consultants and staffed by the

Ancient Monuments secretariat. The new body is interested not only in identifying and in listing but in keeping records. Increasingly, evidence derived from industrial archaeology will be related to evidence derived from other sources, and this in itself is voluminous. Of course, none of these interests can guarantee preservation. There are so many industrial sites in Britain, many of them located in areas where for quite different reasons preservation is difficult, that, as Kenneth Hudson puts it, 'it is neither realistic nor desirable to try to preserve more than a small proportion of our surviving stock of obsolete buildings and equipment'. Ironbridge remains a very special case.

Meanwhile, the study of industrial archaeology continues to draw on local interest. *The Industrial Archaeology of the British Isles* volumes, edited by E. R. R. Green, bring this out clearly. An excellent example from the series, Frank Atkinson's *North East England* (1974), starts where much of the story covered in this volume begins. Atkinson is Director of Beamish, the new North of England Regional Open Air Museum in County Durham, a key stop in any tour of industrial Britain, past or present. He has ranged widely over his region, building up collections of artefacts and information as well as machines, and these are as essential to an understanding of industrialization (see Chapter IV) as the sites and what was built upon them. The images of industry are of many kinds, and they include both the artefacts and people's sense of the messages they conveyed.

O. G. S. Crawford, founder of *Antiquity*, used to argue that 'archaeology is merely the past tense of anthropology'. The new social history recognizes this. So, too, do the wisest industrial archaeologists. The architect Robert Clough in his *The Lead Smelting Mills of the Yorkshire Dales* (1962), a study of lost industry in a rural setting, began with a survey and ended with a human interpretation. 'As the survey was gradually completed', he wrote, 'it became clear that a most unusual and interesting group of buildings was being recorded for the first time, buildings of honest form and simple character, basically unaffected by any past styles. However, I feel that the book is very much more than a record of stones and mortar: it is a record of a way of life illustrated by certain buildings which were necessary to make that way of life possible. I have endeavoured to look into the lives of these people, at all times somewhat aloof; people who lived, worked and died unnoticed in their remote surroundings.'

The word 'remote' obviously carries many meanings. Some of them will be explored in the chapters which follow. Barrie Trinder chose as the title of his anthology of visitors' impressions of Ironbridge, Coalbrookdale and the Shropshire Coalfield *The Most Extraordinary District in the World*. It was a phrase from a book by a Shrewsbury cotton-master, Charles Hulbert, who came from not very far away. And he, too, included the people:

> From Coalport to the Ironbridge, two miles, the river passes through the most extraordinary district in the world: the banks . . . are studded with Iron-works, Brickworks, Boat Building Establishments, Retail Stores, Inns, and Houses, [with] perhaps 150 vessels on the river, actively employed or waiting for cargoes: while hundreds and hundreds of busy mortals are assiduously engaged, melting with the heat of the roaring furnace; and though enveloped in thickest smoke and incessant dust are cheerful and happy.

How did he know?

The romantic view of industry

2, 3 The transformation of the English landscape by industrial buildings and the pollution of the atmosphere are revealed clearly in Francis Nicholson's lithograph (1821), showing the coal-mining district near Wellington, Shropshire. A more gentle treatment of industrial intrusion in the rural scene is adopted by J.W. Carmichael in a sepia-wash rendering (1840) of a colliery, with steam-powered winding gear and rail access, in Northumberland.

4, 5 The arduous nature of the working conditions, often extremely hot and unpleasant, associated with newly developing industrial processes is not immediately obvious in these interiors: 'drawing the retorts at the great gas-light establishment, Brick Lane' (i.e. raking coke from the ovens), as depicted in a coloured aquatint (1821) by Colin MacKenzie; and an ironworks at Middlesbrough, as seen in a sepia-wash study (1865) for an oil-painting by A. Hunt.

Traditional sources of power

6 A team of horses was used for the repeated raising of the captive grooved hammer of a 'new engine for driving piles'; on reaching a certain point the gripping device was forced open to release the hammer. Engraving from J. T. Desaguliers, *The Course of Experimental Philosophy*, 1745.

7 Manpower in the literal sense was utilized in this dredger for clearing harbours; equipped with two buckets, the vessel (used at Dunkirk and Toulon) was operated by a master supervising three men and two boys who drove the large and small treadwheels, and accompanied by two boats to remove the mud and sand dredged from depths of up to 30 ft. Engraving, characteristic of its period, from Charles Vallancey's *A Treatise on Inland Navigation*, 1763.

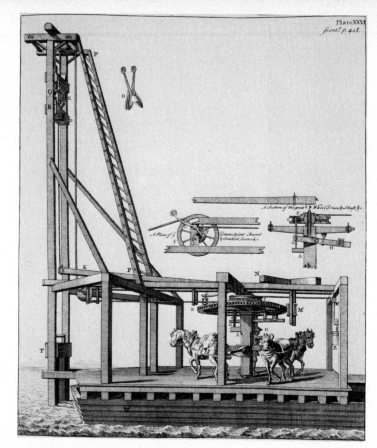

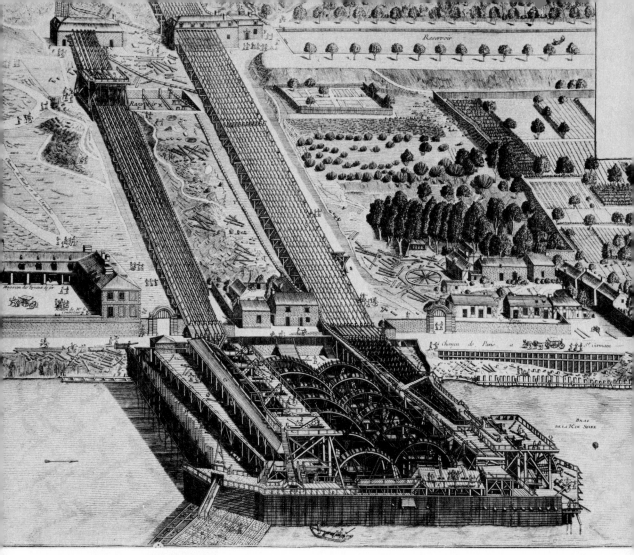

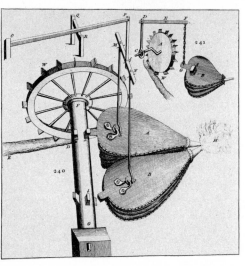

8 The 'Machine de Marly', completed in 1682, utilized the river current to drive the complex set of water-wheels necessary for pumping water from the Seine up to an aqueduct (not shown here) leading to the Palace of Versailles; in this way a regular supply could be provided for the lakes and fountains in the palace gardens. This anonymous engraving demonstrates the contemporary fascination with complicated equipment.

9 Another use of a water-wheel was to drive a set of twin-bellows which were depressed by cogs to provide a continuous draught to a furnace or other fire (marked 'H'); the bellows were automatically raised and opened by a separate system ('O-P') in readiness for the next blast of air.

The ENGINE for Raising Water (with a power made) by Fire

10 The atmospheric steam-engine was invented *c.* 1705 by Thomas Newcomen and used mainly for pumping water out of mines. This type of beam-engine was operated indirectly by the creation of a vacuum in the cylinder ('c') which was filled with steam, thus drawing the beam down; this movement, constantly repeated, produced the pumping action. Engraving by H. Beighton, 1717.

11 Newcomen's steam-engine was studied by visiting mechanics and copied abroad: this engraving, showing one such example at Dannemora in Sweden, is taken from a publication of 1734 by Marten Triewald, who had returned home in 1726 after spending ten years in England.

12 *Below.* James Watt's invention in 1782 of a rotary engine directly powered by steam pressure provided the means of turning a shaft and thus operating machinery. This Boulton and Watt engine, installed at the Albion Mill, Blackfriars (see p. 141), is a development of Watt's design and incorporates all the major design features patented by Watt: separate condenser; parallel motion; and the 'sun and planet' gears.

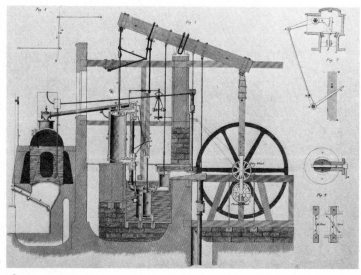

13 George Stephenson's own drawing of his locomotive built in 1814 for use on the Killingworth Colliery wagonway.

14 The *Enterprise*, a steam-carriage providing a passenger service in London, *c.* 1830.

Early industrialization in Shropshire

15 A detail of John Rocque's map of the county (1752), showing the Severn Gorge. The centre of Coalbrookdale – which grew considerably in subsequent years – is just north of Benthall Edge, on the opposite side of the river.

Opposite

18 A view of the Severn Gorge, looking west towards the Iron Bridge; this pencil drawing, dated 25 September 1789, was sketched ten years after the completion of the bridge.

19 A view of Coalbrookdale in the 1890s, showing industrial buildings belonging to the Coalbrookdale Company.

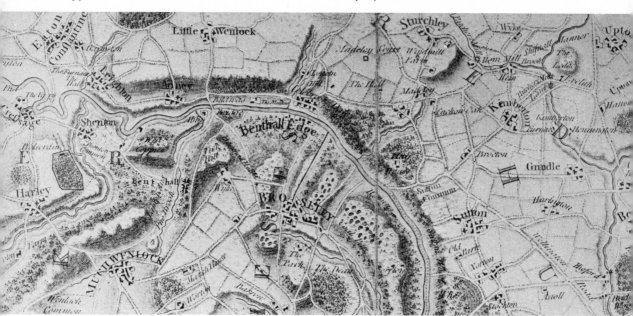

16 The Blists Hill furnaces, here shown in a photograph taken *c.* 1890, were in active use until 1912; they occupy the site formerly owned by the Madeley Wood Company from 1832, and now vested in the care of the Ironbridge Gorge Museum Trust.

17 A Newcomen-type engine, constructed at Heslop, in a photograph taken *c.* 1864; this engine is unusual in that it has been adapted from reciprocating to rotary motion (cf. *ills. 10–12*).

How the early works of industry changed the English landscape

20 The Duke of Bridgewater's canal, designed by James Brindley, was built to carry coal-barges from the Duke's Worsley Colliery to Manchester; the Barton Aqueduct (opened in July 1761) across the River Irwell is seen here in an engraving published in 1785.

21 Prior Park, near Bath, with the iron wagonway laid by Ralph Allen *c.* 1730 to bring stone from his quarries for the major development of the city then being undertaken; engraving by A. Walker, 1750.

Below
22 A fully-laden coal-wagon descending a colliery wagonway at Newcastle; engraving after a drawing by William Beilby, 1773.

Opposite
23 A view of the Calder Valley in Yorkshire, with the industrial town of Sowerby Bridge at the centre, by A.F. Tait, 1845.

24 Wakefield in Yorkshire, seen from a point near Nelson's Foundry; in this lithograph, *c.* 1840, a train can be seen (right, background) leaving the town.

From industrial landscape to industrial wasteland

25 The Iron Forge between Dolgelli and Barmouth, Merionethshire, by Paul Sandby, published in *Welsh Views*, 1776; the water-wheel and the chimney belching smoke are symbolic of the early industrial era.

Below

26 In this view of a mine in South Wales, near Neath, Glamorgan (1798), the presence of a horse gin and a boiler-house should be noted; coloured aquatint by John Hassell.

Opposite

27 The Severn Gorge at Coalbrookdale provides a dramatic setting for 'an iron work[s] for casting cannon' on the north bank; Abraham Darby I began the revival of the local iron industry, and in 1709 developed the use of coke for smelting. Engraving, after a painting by George Robertson, by Wilson Lowry, published in 1788.

28 The landscape despoiled: tin mines at Camborne in Cornwall. This photograph published in 1893 reveals a desolate landscape punctuated by chimneys, each built for a steam-engine used for either pumping or winding operations in an individual shaft.

The fantasy world of steam-power, *c.* 1830

29 'Steam! Steam!! Steam!!!', a lithograph used as a title-page illustration for a song with piano accompaniment, as sung at the Vauxhall pleasure gardens and in music-halls.

30 'The Progress of Steam', an engraving by H. Alken published in 1829.

I say Fellow, give my Buggy a charge of Coke, your Charcoal is so D__d dear.

THE PROGRESS OF STEAM.

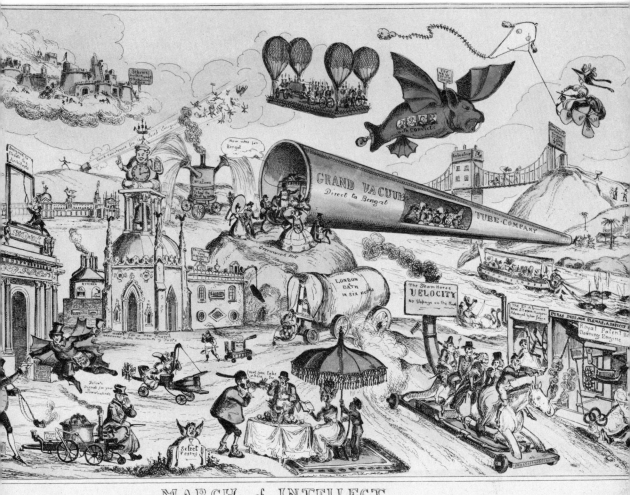

MARCH of INTELLECT

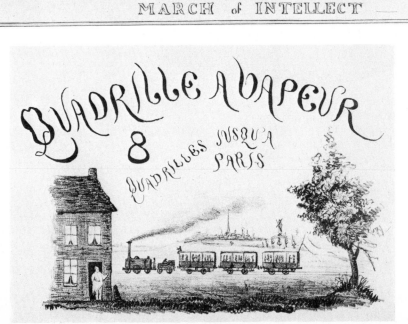

31, 32 Numerous fanciful applications of steam-power are combined in 'March of Intellect', a hand-coloured etching by William Heath (pseudonym, Paul Pry), *c.* 1829; the caption read 'Lord how this world improves as we grow older.' The somewhat unexpected inclusion of a train on the title-page of a piano score adds a novel touch to the 'Quadrille à vapeur' published at Lille.

THAMES TUNNEL 1200FT L^{NG}
COMMENCED 1824 BROKE IN 1828
RECOMMENCED 1835
OPENED TO PEDESTRIANS 1843

33 The Thames Tunnel was the first ever built beneath the soft bed of a river (cf. *colour pl. I*); the reverse of this commemorative medallion (enlarged $2\frac{1}{2}$ times) shows the twin entrances at the Rotherhithe end, and records the main dates associated with the construction – including the collapse and flooding of the works in 1828. Queen Victoria visited the Tunnel in 1843, shortly after its opening.

FOR ALL the changes in historiography and in the contemporary social and cultural context, it is still fashionable among historians to consider the industrial revolution mainly in terms of its economic variables and their interrelationships, with increasing attention being paid to measurement and to the elucidation of the basic fact that so much could happen to the economy within a short period of time without 'the experiment' or the experience being controlled. Even this approach has its images, however. Foreign trade has long been described as an 'engine of growth', and from 1960 onwards it became almost impossible to discuss industrialization without mentioning 'take-off', W. W. Rostow's metaphor derived from more recent technology.

It is possible instead, however, to begin a study of the industrial revolution in terms of particular places and their particular inter-relationships. This was an approach much favoured by the late C. R. Fay, and its attractions have increased in the light of more recent work both by local historians and by industrial archaeologists. The unification of England, let alone the unification of Britain, should never be taken for granted, and an industrial revolution was required before it was possible to talk of a 'British economy', a term which Rostow took for granted. Prices (and wages) varied from one district to another: so, too, did output. What happened at Coalbrookdale – or for that matter in London or Liverpool – could not be held to be 'typical'. The linkages came through a growing home market – Coalbrookdale benefited directly here – and from the expansion (not least through turnpikes and canals) of the distribution network. When Josiah Wedgwood turned to canal-building, he attached great importance to those inland towns and cities which had a stake in canals, to make formal overtures to the Corporation of Liverpool. Turnpike politics, too, took up a great deal of time, as road improvements (associated with names like blind Jack Metcalfe and J. L. Macadam) were canvassed. There were banking and credit linkages, too, through the development of the country banking system. Yet contrasts persisted. It was after the Napoleonic Wars that William Cobbett viewed and described such contrasts in *Rural Rides*, as he made his way along the winding roads of England. Many of the contrasts were still there in the 'age of the Chartists', twenty years or more later.

Whether we begin with variables or places, however, we face the same complexities of time-span. Just as economic historians dealing in variables have come to the conclusion, as R. M. Hartwell has put it, that the 'forces making for growth' in the eighteenth century were not autonomous variables, but 'manifestations of growth itself', self-sustaining growth with a large and complex history, so historians of place must go back long before the industrial revolution. Before cotton, there was wool. Before Bradford in Yorkshire there was Bradford-on-Avon in Wiltshire. Before the full development of the Black Country, there was the prosperous iron industry of Sussex. As early as the 1580s, Camden had described Sussex as 'full of iron mines'. 'Many streams', he went on, 'are drawn into one channel, and a great deal of meadow ground is turned into ponds and pools for the driving of mills by the flashes, which, beating with hammers upon the iron, fill the neighbourhood round about it, day and night, with continual noise.' Decline began in the 1650s, but the sole remaining forge and furnace continued to work at Ashburnham near Battle until the 1820s.

There were other areas which were increasingly 'industrial'. Sussex had depended on timber, and as at early Coalbrookdale, timber and iron seemed to go together as coal and iron were to do later. 'Nature has thought fit to produce this wasting ore more plentifully in woodlands than any other ground and to enrich our forests to their own destruction', wrote the diarist John Evelyn in 1664. The Forest of Dean, where there was local coal, was heavily cut over. One of the most interesting development areas was the North-East, and it was in the seventeenth century, not the eighteenth, that a poet could write:

> England's a perfect world, hath Indies too;
> Correct your maps, Newcastle is Peru.

Coal was being carried then by sea to London in what seemed to be huge quantities from the Newcastle and Durham coalfields, the first to be developed on a large scale. Northern squires fully appreciated where the priorities lay. 'But what signifie all your Balls, Ridottos etc. unless Navigation and the Coal Trade flourish?', asked Sir Henry Liddell Bt in 1729. Four years earlier he had joined in an agreement to limit coal production in order to maintain coal prices in the metropolis. Even in the seventeenth century, London had been so smoky that the diarist John Evelyn had compared dark London with 'the picture of Troy sacked by the Greeks, or the approaches of Mount-Hecla'.

The North-East had many industrial establishments early in the eighteenth century, and it was there that new techniques and new forms of organization were tried out. Ambrose Crowley had begun to set up huge forges, foundries and slitting mills there in the late-seventeenth century, using water-power. Steel goods were one of his specialities, and it was not until Benjamin Huntsman had developed new techniques for making cast or crucible steel that Sheffield moved far ahead in the late eighteenth century. (Yet Defoe had described Sheffield, centre of an old metal handicrafts district, as 'very populous and large', and its houses were said to be 'dark and black' from the smoke of the forges.) The glass trade flourished in the North-East, too, as a by-product of the coal trade, and on Tyneside alone by 1772 there were numerous specialist workshops manufacturing glass: broad window glass (five); glass bottles (five); crown glass (three); flint glass (two); and plate glass (one). The printing trade was prosperous, and more children's books were produced in Newcastle during the 1770s than in any city except London.

Coal was the foundation of everything else, however, and it was development in coal-mining that stimulated the beginnings of the transport revolution. Colliery wagonways were in use early in the eighteenth century – with horses drawing coal to the riverside. (The first iron rails were contemplated sixty years before those at Coalbrookdale.) Some of the wagonways demanded the construction of huge arches, bridges and embankments. Thus, the Beckley Burn Embankment, several hundred yards long, some 100 ft high and 300 ft broad at the centre (1725),

22

and the Causey Arch, semicircular and over 100 ft in span, are two superb early industrial monuments on Tanfield Moor in County Durham.

Soon after the beginning of the nineteenth century, stationary steam-engines were brought into operation, winding sets of wagons from collieries below. (The last steam-haulage engine did not go out of use until 1960.) Not surprisingly, there was an early interest in locomotives also: a locomotive to Trevithick's design was built at Gateshead in 1805, though never used; and George Stephenson had seen several locomotives before he produced his own, the *Blücher*, in 1814. That was eleven years before his *Locomotion* drew a load of coal- and passenger-wagons on the Stockton and Darlington Railway.

During the nineteenth century, Newcastle and Tyneside were to become great world centres of shipbuilding – iron ships were being built in the 1840s and the Jarrow Shipyard was opened in 1852, one year after the Great Exhibition – but in this case, too, the foundations of shipbuilding were prepared long before. Coal made its way south before the railways in coastal colliers, for the most part owned by people or interests outside Tyneside; and until steam-power was introduced to the Tyne in 1822 with the first paddle-tugs, the tough, traditional keelmen carried out the arduous task of transporting coal from the staithes to the colliers.

If the North-East was one of Samuel Smiles's 'development areas', but an area with a long history, the South-West – outward-looking because of its seamen, its fishermen and its traders – also had its own traditional industrial pattern which preceded the industrial revolution. Its tin-mines were known in the ancient world, and in the eighteenth century Trevithick's father was a mine manager. Of the great names of the early history of industrial England, indeed, Thomas Savery was born in 1650 at Plymouth, Thomas Newcomen in 1663 at Dartmouth, Henry Cort (who revolutionized iron-making in the 1780s by the invention of the processes of puddling and rolling) at Portsmouth in 1740, and Humphry Davy, inventor of the safety-lamp, at Penzance in 1778. There were no big towns in Cornwall, however, and the area never developed the relationship with London 'enjoyed' by the North-East. One interdependence became increasingly significant in the eighteenth century. China clay was transported from Cornwall – the extraction of clay left 'lunar' landscapes – to the Potteries in the northern Midlands. Josiah Wedgwood, indeed, made his own works almost independent of local supplies of raw materials. An impetus was given, thereby, to the building of canals. Wedgwood was an enthusiastic supporter of the Grand Trunk Canal which linked the Potteries with the Mersey in the North, the Midlands and London, and his Etruria Works were served directly by barges laden with china clay and coal.

The Potteries were a distinctive new industrial area, which, like the other industrial areas, continued to blend town and country, although the anonymous historian of the *History of the Staffordshire Potteries* (1829) claimed that 'the Art was practised here during the time the country was tributary to the Roman power'. Henry Wedgwood, second son of Josiah Wedgwood I, wrote in six volumes *The Romance of Staffordshire* and *Staffordshire Up and Down the County*, based on 'sketches' originally contributed to Staffordshire newspapers. 'The love of Country, next to the love of the Creator,' he wrote, 'is the noblest feeling cherished by man.' Hills and kilns go together in his sketches. Other writers from outside the

Map showing the development of industrialization in Britain in 1815; a notable feature is the concentration of manufacturing industries in areas having a plentiful supply of iron and coal, combined with access to facilities for transporting materials and goods by water.

35

Potteries, notably Professor W. G. Hoskins, have seen only ugliness there – 'a formless landscape, usually thickly blanketed with smoke', with derelict land and 'homes intermingled with filthy potbanks'. To Hoskins, indeed, the Potteries and the Black Country foreshadowed 'the landscape of Hell'.

The 'Black Country' had a long industrial history, and as early as 1617 Yarranton claimed that there were more people living within a radius of ten miles of Dudley (in Worcestershire) and more 'money returned in a year' than in four Midland farming counties. Although the description 'Black Country' had not then been invented, the countryside was in the process of becoming industrialized. Visitors there could see what Professor W. H. B. Court, in his fascinating book *The Rise of the Midland Industries* (1938), called 'a strung-out web of iron-working villages, market-towns next door to collieries, heaths and wastes gradually and very slowly being covered by the cottages of nailers and other persons carrying on industrial occupations in rural surroundings'.

South Staffordshire was rich in coal and iron, and the industrialists of the late eighteenth century who worked the mines and the metals were just as interested in canal-building as were Wedgwood and the great potters. 'Thick coal' was exploited increasingly as the century went by, with the town of Wednesbury being renowned for the quality of its coal: the iron-ores, also worked in Wednesbury, were not of a high grade, but they were much in demand. There were other extractive industries, too: Stourbridge clay, for example, was used by Abraham Darby I at Coalbrookdale and at the end of the century by Huntsman in Sheffield. In return, pig-iron was imported from Coalbrookdale as the demand for iron increased.

The extractive industries were only the base of the local economy, however, which depended for its expansion on a wide range of manufacturing skills. Nailmaking, 'the handloom weaving' of the Black Country, was only the first of them. It was in the Black Country, near Dudley, that Newcomen erected the first steam-engine with a piston and cylinder in 1712. It was in the Black Country that John Wilkinson opened up the Bilston district, building a blast-furnace in 1758 and a forge for producing wrought iron in 1782. His passion for iron was shared by others, although they did not always express it so articulately in words. In 1796 there were fourteen blast-furnaces in the Black Country, in 1830 there were 123. After 1832 the first square blast-furnaces began to go out of use – following an invention of John Gibbons – and blast-furnaces were built in a style which continued throughout the century. Meanwhile, new puddling techniques were developed. By 1850 the iron industry was on the eve of its peak prosperity, although fears were soon being expressed about the future exhaustion of supplies of both iron and coal.

Already when Queen Victoria came to the throne in 1837, the Black Country was known as such – ugly buildings, smoky new towns, and mazes of roads and canals with railways soon to come. (The earliest main line in the area, the Grand Junction, was opened in 1837.) The 'uncounted steam engines' had 'tall chimneys' bristling 'the surface of the district', as one local writer put it. In the 1843 Report of the Midland Mining Commission, Thomas Tancred was more eloquent:

> The traveller appears never to get out of an interminable village, composed of cottages and very ordinary houses. In some directions he may travel for miles, and never be out of sight of numerous two-storied

houses; so that the area covered by bricks and mortar must be immense.
These houses, for the most part, are not arranged in continuous streets but are interspersed with blazing furnaces, heaps of burning coal in process of coking, piles of ironstone calcining, forges, pit-banks, and engine chimneys; the country being intersected with canals, crossing each other at different levels; and the small remaining patches of the surface soil occupied with irregular fields of grass or corn, intermingled with heaps of the refuse of mines or slag from the blast furnaces. Sometimes the road passes between mounds of refuse from the pits, like a deep cutting on a railway: at others it runs like a causeway, raised some feet above the fields on either side, which have subsided by the excavation of the minerals beneath . . . The whole country might be compared to a vast rabbit warren. It is a matter of everyday occurrence for houses to fall down, or a row of buildings inhabited by numerous families to assume a very irregular outline . . . caused by the sinking of the ground into old workings.

The passage should be compared with Charles Dickens's account in *The Old Curiosity Shop*, written two years earlier:

On every side and as far as the eye could see into the heavy distance, tall chimneys, crowding on each other . . . poured out their plague of smoke. . . . On mounds of ashes by the wayside, sheltered only by a few rough boards, or rotten pent-house roofs, strange engines spun and writhed like tortured creatures . . . making the ground tremble with their agonies.

The Black Country was closely linked with Birmingham, one of the great industrial cities which will be described later, along with its counterparts. Yet there were contrasts as well as complementarities. The dialect was different. So, too, was the humour. The social structure was distinctive: so, too, were ways of leisure. A strong sense of place – and of belonging – was as marked as it was in the Potteries. Staffordshire was a kind of kingdom in miniature in the nineteenth century – with the Black Country in the south, with Birmingham links; the Potteries in the north, with Manchester and Pennine links; and fields and farms in between. The scarred landscapes bound people together. It was not felt to be surprising that people 'consistently employed in mining and in blackening manufactures, united but little with society beyond their own narrow circuits, should acquire or preserve – peculiarity of manner, habit and language'. The 'peculiar' ways persisted with the scars. It was in 1915 not in 1855 that a distinguished geographer wrote that 'the whole district is one great workshop, both above ground and below. At night it is lurid with the flames of iron furnaces; by day it appears one vast loosely-knit town of humble homes, amid cinder-heaps and fields stripped of vegetation by smoke and fumes.'

This was one cluster of images of industry, directly related to places. There was a second equally important cluster, however, associated not with coal and iron but with textiles. There had been a long history of textile production in England – Professor Carus-Wilson, indeed, identified an industrial revolution in the thirteenth century associated with the application of water-power to clothmaking. The woollen-textiles industry at the beginning of the eighteenth century depended as much on running water as on wool. 'At every considerable house was a manufactory or work-house', Daniel Defoe said of the country near Halifax in the West Riding of Yorkshire in the early eighteenth century, 'and as they could not do their business without water the little streams were so parted and guided by gutters and pipes, and by turning and dividing the streams, that none of these houses were without a river, if I may call it so, running into and through their work-houses.'

Defoe noted the presence of coal in the area also. ('Every clothier kept a horse or two, to carry his coal from the pit, to fetch home his wool and his provisions from the market, to take his yarn to the weavers, his cloth to the fulling mill and finally to the cloth market to be sold.') There were textile areas in England on the eve of the industrial revolution, however, where there was no coal. Defoe saw 'a Face of Diligence spread over the whole country' in East Norfolk with 'vast manufactures', and in the West of England, where Wiltshire, Somerset and Gloucester were all rich centres of clothmaking, with widely scattered towns. Even Devonshire seemed to Defoe to 'be so full of great Towns, and those Towns so full of people and those People so universally employ'd in Trade and Manufactures, that not only it cannot be equall'd in England, but perhaps not in Europe'; and the serge market in Exeter 'next to the Brigg-Market at Leeds in Yorkshire is the greatest in England'.

46

Woollen textiles from the West of England held their own during the early years of industrialization; so that it could be written of the Chalfond Valley in Gloucestershire as late as 1824:

> With handsome mills this craggy dell doth teem,
> Where engines work by water and by steam.

'The clothing industry is so eminent in this county,' Sir Robert Atkyns had told a correspondent in 1712, 'that no other manufacture deserves a mention'. Australian wool made a difference. So also did the rise of the cotton industry, which developed faster – a hare among tortoises – than any other textile industry. When a knowledgeable student of textiles could write in 1821 that he had seen some fine cloths made from Australian wools – 'there is great kindness in the wool' – the writing was on the wall. Cotton had already leapt ahead. The net import of raw cotton into England had been about 6 million lb a year in the period 1776–81: in 1782–4 it was nearly double, and in 1785–8 more than treble that figure. A cheaper, more flexible material had won the day, and in the wake of the victory came the mills and the machines.

36, XX

Richard Arkwright, the most assertive of the new cotton men, built his first spinning mill, driven by horses, at Nottingham, an old textiles centre – and home of the stocking-frame – in 1768; his second factory, however, built at Cromford on the River Derwent in Derbyshire in 1771, was driven by water-power. It was a magnificent factory, painted by Joseph Wright, and it was widely imitated. 'We all looked up to him', the first Sir Robert Peel said of Arkwright, 'and imitated his mode of building.' Appropriately, the Derwent Valley soon had the largest concentration of mills in the country, mills where Arkwright's workers could sing:

> Come let us all here join in one,
> And thank him for all favours done;
> Let's thank him for all favours still
> Which he hath done beside the mill.

When Arkwright died in 1792 at the age of fifty-nine he left, in the words of *The Gentleman's Magazine*, 'manufactories the income of which is greater than that of most German principalities'.

If Derbyshire led the way – and Milford, just south of Belper, a factory town fashioned by the Strutts, remains a complete and almost untouched industrial village – Lancashire became the world-renowned centre of the cotton industry – with ancillary mills and warehouses in Scotland (including Robert Owen's New Lanark) and many other parts of England. On the eve of the arrival of cotton in 1777, Preston, an ancient town, was a 'genteel' place. Soon it was one town among many, one of the sources of inspiration for Dickens's 'Coketown'. Writing about the great transformation in 1892, L. H. Grindon remarked 'A "Lancashire scene" has been said to resolve into "bare hills and chimneys"; and as regards the cotton districts the description is, upon the whole, not inaccurate. Chimneys predominate innumerably in the landscape, a dark pennon usually undulating from every summit – perhaps not pretty pictorially, but in every case a gladsome sight, since it means work, wages, food, for those below, and a fire upon the hearth at home. . . . The smoke denotes human happiness for thousands: when her chimneys are smokeless, operative Lancashire is hungry and sad.' The mill chimneys of the area round Stalybridge were almost like a forest, and there were some magnificent factories.

There were parts of the West Riding which were not dissimilar after steam-power had been applied to the woollen and worsted industries in the early nineteenth century. George Walker's description of 1814 should be compared with that of Defoe. 'A great part of the West Riding of Yorkshire abounds with . . . mills, . . . manufactories and other large buildings appropriate to trade, which are now usually known under the general, though perhaps vulgar denomination of factories. They are essentially requisite for a widely extended Commerce of Britain, and furnish employment, food and raiment to thousands of poor, industrious individuals. It is much, however, to be lamented that this is too frequently at the expense of health and morals.'

It is impossible to describe the appearance of the textile districts without lingering longer on the factories. The word was new, but the concept had been anticipated in 1718–22 in the Derby silk-mill, five or six storeys high, which was built for John and Thomas Lombe. It employed 300 men, and was vividly described in 1836, when the whole of 'this elaborate machine' was 'put in motion by a simple water-wheel'. In 1741 Lewis Paul used donkey power in a pioneering Birmingham cotton factory and a year later built a mill using water-power at Northampton (with the support of the Editor of *The Gentleman's Magazine*). Arkwright's great mill at Cromford provided a model, but there was considerable variety in external decoration and design features. Thus, at Leeds, for example, John Marshall built a flax-mill in 1840 with the appearance of an ancient Egyptian temple. The first chimney, built in the form of an obelisk in imitation of Cleopatra's Needle, cracked in 1852 and was replaced by a more conventional structure. Disraeli gave his own guise to the mill in his novel *Sybil* (1844), where he described it as 'one of the marvels of the district; one might also say of the country'. He dwelt on the idea that mill-owners need not only be concerned with profits: they could be proud of their 'order'.

51

48

There were obvious limitations to such an assessment (see Chapter III) and Marx, drawing on the experiences of his friend Friedrich Engels in Manchester, sharply criticized Andrew Ure's *The Philosophy of Manufactures* (1835) where *inter alia* factories were described as 'magnificent edifices, surpassing far in number, value, usefulness and ingenuity of construction, the boasted monuments of Asiatic, Egyptian, and Roman despotism'. Arkwright had led the way, Ure claimed, with the 'verve and ambition' of Napoleon.

Some of the factories were 'models', although others were noisy, crowded, dark and thoroughly unpleasant to work in. The 'factory system', a new term of the 1830s, was often identified not only with novelty but with tyranny. The model factories were often found in small textile villages and towns on both sides of the Pennines. Indeed, Arkwright's partners, the Strutts, had led the way in eighteenth-century Belper: there were 300 company cottages there by 1830. Samuel Oldknow, who raised a mortgage from Arkwright, developed a new community round his mill at Mellor in Cheshire (1787), diversifying employment: he even built a boarding-house. Thomas Ashton's Hyde in Lancashire was warmly praised by Léon Faucher, the explorer from across the Channel who was fascinated by English industrialization. 'At the beginning of the present century', he wrote in 1844, Hyde was 'a little hamlet, of only 800 souls, on the summit of a barren hill, the soil of which did not yield enough for the inhabitants. The brothers Ashton have peopled and enriched this desert. Ten thousand people are now established in their five factories. . . . The houses inhabited by the work-people form long and large streets. . . . Each house contains upon the ground floor a sitting room, a kitchen and a back-yard, and above are two or three bedrooms.'

Other 'model' communities, better known, were New Lanark in Scotland, developed but not founded by Robert Owen, and Saltaire near Bradford, Yorkshire's bustling 'Worstedopolis', complete with assembly room, chapel, hospital, school, baths and public wash-house (the mills were opened in 1853). Near Halifax, still a textiles centre, as it had been in the days of Defoe, Colonel Edward Akroyd, Sir Titus Salt's counterpart, built a mill at Copley in 1847 and added 'domestic gothic' terraced cottages (1847–53) with gardens, a school (1849), a library (1850) and a church (1863). This was planned industrialization, as was Akroyd's proudly named new industrial settlement, Akroydon.

The greatest cotton centre, however – by the 1840s more a warehousing and servicing centre than a factory city – was unplanned. Manchester was regarded by contemporaries as a portent. The number of inhabitants of it and neighbouring Salford grew from 25,000 in 1772 to 181,031 in 1821 and 455,153 in 1851. 'Manchester streets may be irregular . . . its smoke may be dense and its mud ultra-muddy,' observed a writer in an 1858 periodical, 'but not all or any of these things can prevent the image of a great city riding before us as the very symbol of civilization, foremost in the grand march of improvement, a grand incarnation of progress.' For more than twenty years visitors both from Britain and from abroad had been travelling to it as if to industrial Mecca. 'The age of ruins is past,' Sidonia tells young Coningsby in Disraeli's novel *Coningsby* (1844). 'Have you seen Manchester?' It was 'the most wonderful city of modern times'. As early as 1821, John Jones, an operative spinner, had written in his poem 'The Cotton Mill':

> Now see the Cotton from the town convey'd
> To Manchester, that glorious mart of trade:
> Hail splendid scene! The Nurse of every Art,
> That glads the widow's and the orphan's heart!
> Thy mills, like gorgeous palaces arise,
> And lift their useful turrets to the skies.

This 'wonderful city' could shock, however, as much as it could inspire, and it was less its wealth which impressed Friedrich Engels than its social divisions which he thought pointed to revolution and a new order of society. The layout of its streets revealed social segregation. From the broad radial roads leading outwards the slums were invisible. 'The manufactories and machine shops form, as it were, a girdle around the town . . . factories seven storeys in height rear their lofty fronts along the banks of the Irwell and along the borders of the canals. . . . The waters of the Irk, black and fetid, . . . supply numerous tanneries and dye-works: those of the Medlock supply calico-printing establishments, machine shops and foundries.' Whatever the establishments, 'invention, physical progress, discovery' were 'the war-cries'. Yet whatever the establishments, there was 'nothing but masters and men'. The social contradictions of early industrial capitalism were never absent. A prophetic note was struck as Manchester was deemed in 1847 to be 'a clue, more or less perfect, to the social condition of the future'.

Certainly the problems were not unique. Across the Pennines, William Osborn read the following poem to the members of the Leeds Philosophical and Literary Society, which also had its well-established and prestigious Manchester counterpart:

> The AIRE below is doubly dyed and damned;
> The AIR above, with lurid smoke is crammed;
> The ONE flows steaming foul as Charon's Styx,
> Its poisonous vapours in the other mix.
> These sable twins the murky town invest, –
> By them the skin's begrimed, the lungs oppressed.
> How dear the penalty thus paid for wealth;
> Obtained through wasted life and broken health;
> The joyful Sabbath comes! that blessed day,
> When all seem happy, and when all seem gay!
> The toil has ceased, and then both rich and poor
> Fly off to Harrogate, or Woodhouse Moor.
> The one his villa and a carriage keeps.
> His squalid brother in a garret sleeps.
> HIGH flaunting forest trees, LOW crouching weeds,
> Can this be Manchester? or is it Leeds?

Manchester was most often compared not with Leeds but with neighbouring Liverpool – and with more distant Birmingham. 'Liverpool is one of the wonders of Britain', wrote Daniel Defoe at a time when it certainly was not. Yet just over a hundred years later, after a great burst of commercial expansion, it could be described not unjustly as 'a quondam village' which had become fit to be a 'proud capital for any empire in the world'. Its population grew from just over 4,000 in 1700 to nearly 250,000 in 1841 and nearly 400,000 in 1851: indeed, its shipping list at the later date

38
42

was almost as long as its list of inhabitants at the beginning of the eighteenth century. According to H. Smithers, it was spread out in 1825 'like another Venice upon the waters . . . intersected by numerous docks . . . the gay scene of elegant amusements'.

Steamboats were used on the Mersey for the first time in the second decade of the nineteenth century (although the *Savannah* arrived there in 1819, having used auxiliary steam-power for part of the voyage from New York). A report in the *Liverpool Courier* in the same year described a speedy voyage of the *Duke of Wellington* from Runcorn to Liverpool, evidence of 'the Perfection to which the navigation of steamboats has been carried and the celerity with which they sail'. Five years later the Dublin/Liverpool Steam Navigation Company came into existence. The first passenger steamship to cross the Atlantic from the English side was the Liverpool-owned *Sirius* which left London for New York in 1838; she ran out of coal and her spars had to be used as fuel to complete the crossing. In the same year, however, the breakthrough of steam over sail came with the transatlantic journeys of the *Royal William*. The *Great Britain* was the first screw steamer with an iron hull to cross the Atlantic from Liverpool –

83 though she was built at Bristol – six years later.

Liverpool's docks were the pride of the country – eight new ones were built between 1815 and 1835 – and, like Manchester, its fortunes, which had once depended on slaves, depended increasingly on cotton. The first sale of raw cotton in Liverpool was 6,720 lb – by auction – in 1757. Imports of cotton into Liverpool increased in the course of the eighteenth century and threefold again between 1820 and 1850 – from $\frac{1}{2}$ million bales to $1\frac{1}{2}$ million.

Liverpool did not carry with it industrial images. Its fine buildings, ranging from the sturdily functional to the grand and ostentatious, were bound to impress, but it was a city of problems as well as of opportunities. Its leading figures – members of commercial dynasties like the Rathbones – lived up to the familiar contrast 'Manchester men: Liverpool gentlemen.' But it was a segregated city with appalling housing conditions (more cellar dwellings than anywhere else) and a frightening health record (although it pioneered in appointing a Medical Officer of Health in 1846). There was much casual employment. It had a huge Irish population – 22 per cent of the local population in 1851 had been born in Ireland – but it had lots of Welsh as well. At times it was torn by sectarian strife, and its politics were turbulent and often corrupt. Comparisons were inevitable. That with Bristol was a matter of pride. 'Of all the towns that I visited', the Baron Dupin, a French visitor, stated in 1825, 'Bristol was the one where the general stagnation was most visible and most alarming.' The comparison with Birmingham was not always as encouraging, whether it was politics or social welfare which was being compared. 'The average size of a court in Birmingham,' wrote a Liverpool philanthropist in 1845, 'is twelve times the average size of a court in Liverpool; whilst in Birmingham no such thing could be discovered as a human being living in a cellar.'

43 Birmingham by then was undoubtedly England's most versatile industrial city, a city not of great mills and warehouses, like Manchester, but of small workshops. 'Masters' and 'men' had closer relations than in the textiles districts, and there was a feeling, at least, that there was far greater social mobility. By the year 1800 Birmingham had emerged as the leading industrial and commercial centre of the Birmingham Plateau, far more important than, for example, the old incorporated city of Coventry, densely packed and dirty, which in 1830 still had only 27,000 inhabitants, or the old cathedral cities of Lichfield and Worcester. (In 1841 the *Coventry Herald* complained that Coventry goods intended for London had to be taken all the way to Birmingham to be put on the train.) The population of Birmingham increased from 70,000 in 1801 to over 130,000 by 1831, and it was employed in a wide range of metal trades, notably guns, jewellery, buttons and brass products. Its first Improvement Act had been passed in 1769, and while one of its first historians, William Hutton, believed (in 1781) that 'a town without a charter is a town without a shackle', consistent improvement policies required basic changes in local government.

One of the key sites of the early industrial revolution, as interesting as Ironbridge and Coalbrookdale, was the Soho site, where Boulton and Watt developed the steam-engine. (Paradoxically, perhaps, it was used more outside Birmingham than within the city.) Leland had described Birmingham in 1558 as 'a good Markett Towne', a great part of which was 'maintained by Smithes, whoe have theire Iron and Sea-Cole out of Staffordshire'. By the late eighteenth century, it was already in the more terse description of Edmund Blake 'the toy shop of Europe'. 'An infinite variety of articles that come under this Denomination are made here. . . .' Boulton was first described as a 'toy maker' – buckles came before steam-engines – and he was prosperous enough in 1772 to tell James Adam that he had 'establish'd a Correspondence in almost every mercantile Town in Europe which regularly supplies me with orders'.

37

The spirit of Soho after the steam-engine is well revealed in the newspaper accounts of the opening of a new foundry in 1796: it had been designed by Peter Ewart, a Manchester millwright who subsequently became the Chief Mechanical Engineer of Portsmouth Dockyard (another of the great sights of the period):

> Two fat sheep (the first fruit of the newly cultivated land of Soho) were sacrificed at the Altar of Vulcan and eaten by the Cyclops in the Great Hall of the Temple which is 46 wide and 100 feet long. . . . When dinner was over, the Founder of Soho entered, and consecrated this new branch of it, by sprinkling the walls with wine, and then in the name of *Vulcan* and of all the gods and goddesses of *Fire* and *Water*, pronounced the name of it Soho Foundry, and all the people cried Amen.

The mythology is as vivid here as it is in the poems of Erasmus Darwin. Yet this was not the only kind of mythology in the new industrial cities. Bradford, which grew from a town of 8,800 in 1760 to 13,264 in 1801 and 66,715 in 1841, looked back to Bishop Blaise. Nottingham, an ancient town, which had been invigorated in the eighteenth century by economic expansion in the Vale of Trent (its population in 1801 was 28,801, and in 1841, 53,091) turned to the mythical 'Ned Ludd' – or, at least, enough disgruntled citizens of Nottingham did – to ensure that the name 'Luddite' passed down into history. Nottingham depended on a backward industry, like a number of other old towns and cities – in this case, the hosiery trade and framework knitting, and it was slow, too, to welcome the railway. The subsequent history of the introduction of the machine-made lace industry demonstrates how difficult it is to generalize about 'textiles'.

It is difficult to generalize about towns and cities also. There were common urban problems, but each town or city had its own economic base, its own social profile and its own cultural chronology. Leicester was smaller in 1851 than Nottingham, not to speak of Oldham (quintessential new industrial town in Lancashire) or Norwich (quintessential old town). Yet new industries were about to come in. There were also some completely new towns, like Crewe and Swindon, products of the railway age. Already by 1842 Crewe was the focus of four lines of railway. 'Nobody seemed to think of going away from the station,' a writer in *Chambers's Edinburgh Journal* remarked in 1850, 'indeed the only mode of exit and entrance was through a close-shut iron gate'. Yet there was in existence 'a mechanical settlement in an agricultural district', dependent on railway works and engine-sheds as well as station, and there was a population of nearly 5,000 in 1851. Swindon, in rural Wiltshire, developed with the Great Western Railway after 1841, a self-contained little town at first. Three hundred cottages were planned, and 243 of them had been completed by 1853 when an epidemic of typhus hit the new community.

50

In economic terms, Wiltshire in the nineteenth century was a county which did not grow fast. Among those which did were the West Riding of Yorkshire and Lancashire, and their great growth had begun in the eighteenth century. By 1801 indeed, 45 per cent of Britain's occupied population already lived in seven large districts, the precursors of the twentieth-century conurbations. At the time of the 1848 Ordnance Survey map large parts of Lancashire, like the Black Country, were already a mesh of converging industry and housing: there was a continuous line of buildings, for example, on the roads between Ashton, Hyde and Dukinfield. In 1700 there had been only 80 to 110 inhabitants to the square mile: a century later there were nearly 400. The total population more than trebled between 1700 and 1900.

By then, Lancashire sustained about 40 per cent of the world's capacity for providing textiles, and there were said to be about as many cotton spindles in the Oldham district alone as in France and Germany together. 'Not only have the manufacturing processes received the careful attention of the cleverest and highest skilled workers,' an observer stated in the *Journal of the Textile Institute* in 1912, 'but the question of the distribution of the finished article has also received the consideration to which its importance entitles it. The network of organisations radiating from Lancashire penetrates to every part of the globe.'

The economy of the cotton-mills – some very large by nineteenth-century standards – and the pride of some, at least, of the mill-owners in their own order received almost as much attention as the industrial vitality of the country. Lancashire, however, was not exclusively dependent on cotton. In the St Helens district, for example, where the first canal in England, the Sankey Brook Navigation, was cut in 1755, coal was followed by glass and chemicals. The first mention of glasshouses on near-by Merseyside had been in 1696: St Helens became prominent almost a century later. By 1830 smoke carrying 'noxious vapours' from the alkali works had blackened the countryside and killed the hedgerows. In 1846 a reporter wrote of the town:

The first view of St. Helens is not very prepossessing. It lies on a piece of level ground surrounded by a few gentle eminences, and seldom on any weekday is it without its overhanging cloud of smoke. Through this the visitor sees irregular masses of brick houses, two or three churches with square towers, tall chimneys vomiting smoke, and conical glass-houses, giving out occasional bright flashes of flame. The clank of hammers ringing against iron is heard from many a forge and foundry and a strange compound of smells proceed from a chemical works which rears its head close by the railway station and in the suburbs of the town. The streets have apparently been laid out without any plan, as chance or interest might direct. . . . In many of the streets only one side has been built up and there are therefore various vacant spaces of ground which, in rainy weather, contain pools of water and prove anything but conducive to health. Like many other manufacturing places, St. Helens seems to have been built in a hurry, the attention of the inhabitants being so absorbed in advancing manufactures that they would care little about the kind of houses they should provide for themselves.

It was places like St Helens and the new town of Middlesbrough (described fully in my *Victorian Cities*; 1963) which seemed to mark the break in English history, and it was easy then and even now to sigh, as the journalist and novelist Sir Philip Gibbs once sighed (*The Way of Escape*; 1933), 'How pleasant a place it might be' if there had been no industrial revolution. 'They rhythm of life would be slower. . . . Everything we used would have the touch of handicraft which no machine can give.' Complaints about the 'hurry' of life had been just as loud during the 1850s. As Matthew Arnold, one of the great complainers, put it in *The Scholar Gipsy*:

> Too rare, too rare, grow now my visits here!
> 'Mid city noise, not, as with thee of yore,
> Thyrsis! in reach of sheep-bells is my home.

The complaints, however moving, ignored part of the facts of life and their aesthetics as well as their economics. Even in St Helens 'much remained that was pleasantly rural. . . . There were still many open spaces and the inhabitants had only to walk a short distance to the "gentle eminences" surrounding the town from the smoke and grime and enjoy the fresh air of the countryside.' Middlesbrough was near to the Cleveland Hills – and to Whitby. The great Lancashire hill Pendle overshadowed the cotton towns of Nelson and Colne. Industrial Keighley in the West Riding was only a few miles from Haworth (itself an industrial village) and the moors: Hebden Bridge was in the moors of Lancashire. It was claimed in 1892 that 'the only portion' of the county of Lancashire 'entirely devoid of landscape beauty is that which is traversed by the Liverpool and Southport Railway, not unjustly regarded as the dullest in the Kingdom. The best that can be said of this dreary district is that, at intervals it is relieved by the cheerful hues of cultivation.'

Key sites

34 This view of Abraham Darby's blast-furnaces at Coalbrookdale in 1758 has the added interest of showing coking operations on the right and a team of horses drawing a wagon carrying a cast-iron cylinder for a Newcomen engine. Engraving by François Vivares.

Opposite
36 *Arkwright's Cotton Mill, Cromford*, a night-time view painted by Joseph Wright of Derby, *c.* 1789; this mill (completed in 1771), standing on the bank of the River Derwent, relied on water-power (cf. *colour plate XX*).

35 Josiah Wedgwood's Etruria Works, near Stoke-on-Trent, were opened in 1769; the name was inspired by ancient Etruscan pottery, the appearance and style of which influenced some Wedgwood wares.

Opposite
37 At the time of its opening in 1762, the Soho manufactory of Matthew Boulton was set in semi-rural surroundings near Birmingham, long since engulfed by the spread of the city.

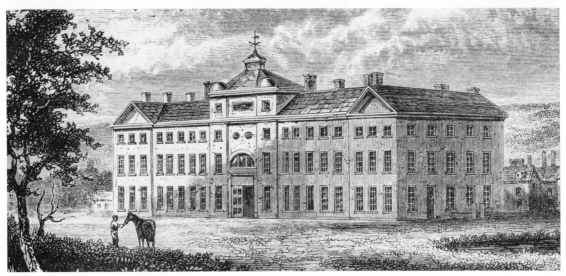

38 Panoramic view of Leeds, from the west, as it
appeared in 1832; the scene is dominated by the many
textile-mills which were the basis of the city's
industrial growth.

39 Bradford, seen from the south-east, in 1841; the
many factory chimneys are associated with the town's
worsted (Bradford was nicknamed 'Worstedopolis')
and woollen industry.

40 *Below*. The construction of a major canal basin, begun in 1768 to link the navigable River Severn with the Staffordshire and Worcester Canal, created in its turn a prosperous town – Stourport – where almost nothing had existed before; this view shows the system of locks in 1776, as seen from the south-west.

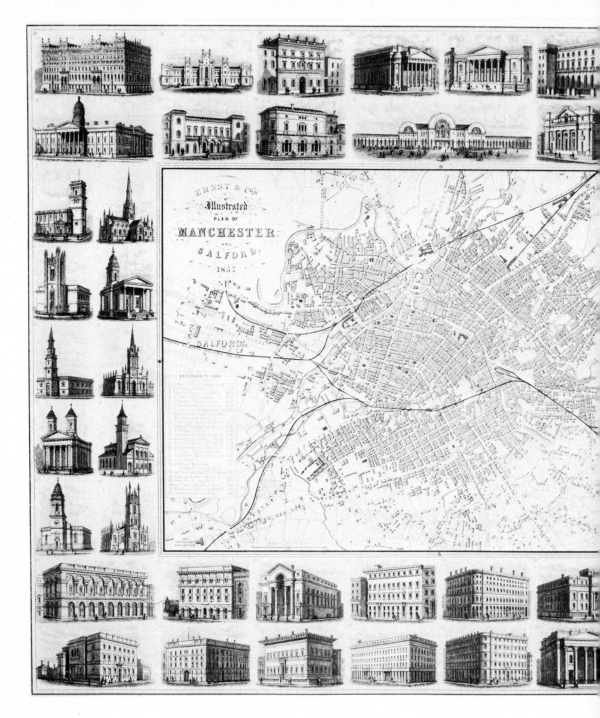

Three cities and their industries

41 An illustrated plan of Manchester and its neighbour, Salford, published in 1857, shows the network of railways which served this major centre of the cotton industry, as well as an impressive array of the city's civic, religious and commercial buildings.

42 Liverpool's docks grew rapidly in the nineteenth century to keep pace with the volume of raw-cotton imports from America, and especially following the introduction of transatlantic steamship services in 1838.

43 Birmingham, the principal industrial and commercial centre of the Midlands, boasted a wide range of small workshops; the banks of the Birmingham Canal Navigation, as seen in this engraving dated 1838, were favoured as the site of many factories and warehouses.

44 The Chelsea Water Works, seen in an engraving published in 1752, employed a pair of Newcomen engines (left) to pump the water-supply for the City of Westminster.

45, 46 In the nineteenth century, new steam-powered textile-mills, such as the Dean Clough Mills at Halifax (right), were easily recognizable, thanks to the tall chimneys of the power-houses. The old-established West of England woollen industry had to be modernized, with the result that industrial buildings, such as the Abbey Cloth Mills at Bradford-on-Avon (below), dominated the small towns in which they were situated.

Opposite
50 The Great Western Railway's locomotive works were situated at a point equidistant from London and Bristol, a choice of location in rural Wiltshire which brought about a planned development at Swindon. This bird's-eye view, looking east, dates from 1849; it shows the clear separation of workshops and rows of houses by the railway.

Industrial buildings in their setting

47 In Birmingham, Messrs Winfield & Sons Manufactory, a complex with canal access (seen in an engraving published in 1861), was one of many associated with metal manufactures – in this case principally bedsteads and gas-fittings.

48, 49 *Above.* One of the features of industrial architecture in England was the incorporation of decorative details harking back to antiquity. One example was Marshall & Co.'s flax-spinning mill in Leeds (top), opened in 1840, which boasted an impressive façade with columns in the Egyptian style. In the U.S.A., however, the cotton-spinning mill built by an English immigrant – Samuel Slater – at Pawtucket, Rhode Island, followed local practice with its use of external timber cladding.

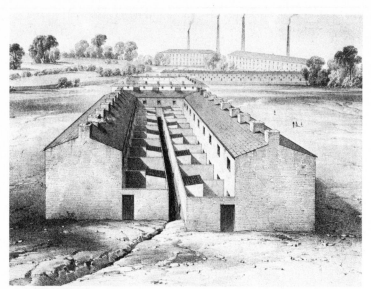

Industrial communities

51, 52 With the rapid growth of industry, the building of factories created a simultaneous need for workers' housing: the terraced back-to-back cottages (with cess-pool drainage) associated with a textile-mill at Preston were illustrated in a report published in 1844. Sir Titus Salt's well-known development, Saltaire, near Bradford – seen here in a modern photograph – dates from 1850.

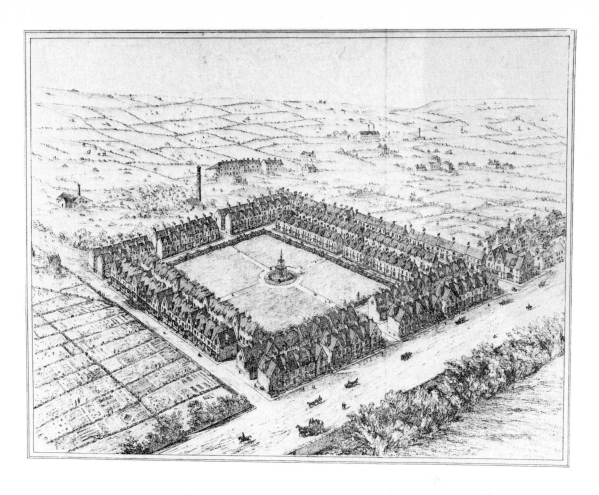

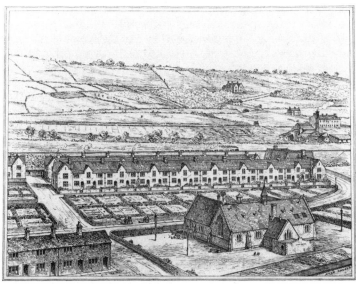

53, 54 Colonel Edward Akroyd was responsible for two notable examples of planned housing associated with industry near Halifax: these engravings, published in 1866, show the type of comprehensive planning – including churches and schools – adopted for the 'model' communities of Akroydon (above) and Copley (left).

Thomas Telford (1759–1834), with his Pont Cysyllte Aqueduct in the background (cf. *ill. 56*); engraving by W. Raddon after the painting by Samuel Lane, 1831.

Canals had often greatly improved the landscape, and they had changed the feel of towns and villages also. The little village of Worsley, for example, was transformed by James Brindley's historic Worsley to Manchester Canal (1760–1) so that for Josiah Wedgwood it had the appearance in 1773 of a 'considerable Seaport town'. (The Canal had also halved the price of coal in Manchester.) As the canals increased, Stourport (at the confluence of the Rivers Stour and Severn) emerged as a beautiful canal town. Before 1772 there had been nothing there but an ale-house: soon it had beautiful Georgian houses and impressive 'functional' buildings. Much of the engineering work on the canals enhanced the sense of place. Lancaster, for example, was given a beautiful aqueduct by John Rennie to carry the Lancaster Canal over the River Lune. Another magnificent example was Telford's Pont Cysyllte aqueduct, carrying the Ellesmere Canal over 100 ft above the Dee Valley. There were some magnificent tunnels, too, and many once-busy inns called 'The Navigation' or just 'The Canal'.

Today, canals are associated with leisurely ways of life – even with leisure – while railways still suggest 'hurry'. Yet it was canals which pointed to the economic advantages of cheap transport before the railway age. J. Phillips, in his *Treatise on Inland Navigation* (1875), remarked sensibly that canals 'highly benefit the manufactures where they have taken place and they occasion the establishment of many new ones'. There were some areas which directly depended on canals for their growth, notably the Birmingham Plateau, and there were few parts of the country where rivers – or roads – were adequate. (Interestingly, St Helens led the way by promoting the 1755 Act for 'making navigable the River Brook called Sankey Brook, and three rural Branches thereof from the River Mersey'.) By the 1820s there were 3,000 miles of canal. There was no 'system': locks, widths and depths of canals varied, and the weather (and the state of the rivers) continued to influence what movement could take place and when. The canal companies were not carriers but toll-takers (although an Act of 1845 allowed them to act as carriers), and the tolls they charged were often too high. Not surprisingly, there was something of a railway take-over. In three years – 1846, 1847 and 1848 – 948 miles of canal passed into the hands of the railways. 'The downfall of the canal industry in the face of the competing railway,' L. T. C. Rolt has written, 'was as swift as its meteoric rise to prosperity'.

Railways were more than arteries, as the canals had been, for everything had to be determined by timetable. A railway *system* was even more necessary than a factory system. William Huskisson, the politician, was killed on the opening day of the Liverpool and Manchester Railway because he misjudged the speed of the train. Relying on the speed of the train soon became a necessary element in all business dealings. Bradshaw, the basic railway timetable, first appeared in 1839. The enormous passenger demand had not been clearly foreseen. Passenger receipts on the Liverpool and Manchester Railway were more than double the freight receipts until 1845. It was an exaggeration completely in character, however, for the Duke of Wellington, who had been present at the opening, to complain that railways enabled 'the lower orders to go uselessly wandering about the country'.

Yet Bradshaw and Blacklock, the original publishers of the great railway guide, also produced superb coloured lithographs, one of Stockport

Viaduct serving as a coloured illustration in Klingender's book; and it is impossible to judge railways solely by their contribution to 'hurry'. They lowered costs and stimulated employment in many industries (particularly iron and coal) and raised the standard of living by improving patterns of distribution. Their straightforward economic significance was immense. That is why local interests took them up so enthusiastically, sometimes too enthusiastically. (The Stockton and Darlington line, like Coalbrookdale a Quaker project, paid dividends of $2\frac{1}{2}$ per cent in 1826, 8 per cent in 1832–3 and 15 per cent in 1839–41, and the price of shares rose from £100 in 1826 to £260 in 1838.) By 1845 a 'railway mania was one of the main topics of conversation . . . and speculation', and the London banks had joined in the enterprise. By then the main trunk lines had already been built, and by 1851 some 6,800 miles of railway were open. Places which were off the railway suffered, like 'Courcy' in Anthony Trollope's *Dr. Thorne* (1858).

Trollope's novels suggest, however, that railways or no railways, industry or no industry, England had not been completely transformed. 'England is not yet a commercial country', he wrote in the same novel, 'in the sense in which that epithet is used for and let us still hope that she will not become so.' Buying and selling might be necessary but they were not 'the noblest work of man'. Fictional 'Barsetshire' survived alongside Lancashire. Other writers made such points more forcibly still – Dickens, for example, and Ruskin. 'So many hundred hands in this mill,' the former wrote of Bounderby's mill in 'Coketown', 'so many hundred horse steam Power. It is known, to the force of a single pound weight, what the engine will do; but not all the calculators of the National Debt can tell me the capacity for good or evil, for love or hatred, for the decomposition of virtue into vice, or the reverse.'

Dickens spent little time in industrial cities, and Ruskin likewise (although he gave two memorable critical addresses in the heart of Bradford). London – with all its problems – was essentially not an industrial city in the mid-nineteenth century; and Ruskin chose eventually to live in the Lake District. None the less, London had large breweries in the eighteenth century, machine-tool shops (like Henry Maudslay's works at Lambeth) in the early part of the nineteenth, and a wide range of consumer industries (like the clothing trades, furniture-manufacture and printing) throughout. The ancient suburb of Spitalfields, moreover, was still employing 7,000 people in the silk trade in the 1840s. 'So rapid is the growth of this queen of cities', wrote a correspondent to *The Builder* in 1844, 'that a population equal to that of Salisbury is added to its numbers every three months; but so overwhelmingly large is this Leviathan of towns, that this constant and progressive increase is scarcely perceived, for it is almost like throwing a bucket of water into the Ocean.'

People wished to escape from London – Dickens was prominent among them – at least as much as from the great new industrial cities, and the map of England contained many places of escape. It is interesting to note that the mill-owner John Marshall's children became country gentlemen living in the Lake District – the main theme of Professor W. G. Rimmer's *Marshall's of Leeds* (1960) – and that a grandson died mountaineering in Switzerland. Matthew Boulton's son had bought the country house and estate of Great Tew in Oxfordshire, one of the most beautiful villages in the country. Richard Cobden, who himself lived at the quiet town of Midhurst in Sussex, complained of the way many mill-owners abandoned their industrial interests and, indeed their economic principles. 'We have the spirit of feudalism rife and rampant in the midst of the antagonistic development of the age of Watt, Arkwright and Stephenson.'

Trollope and Cobden were writing of England, and it is England which is mainly covered in the Elton Collection. What of Scotland and Wales? Both countries had distinct social structures, different religious traditions and great varieties of landscape and resources. Both, too, shared an obvious dependence on improved domestic transport facilities. Samuel Smiles, born in the Scottish Lowlands, wrote a brilliant account of the Scottish Highlands, drawing heavily on Telford. Neither Smiles nor Telford had any sympathy with 'feudalism'. 'I admire commercial enterprise,' wrote Telford. 'It is the vigorous outgrowth of our industrial life: I admire everything that gives it free scope, as wherever it goes, activity, energy, intelligence – all that we call civilization – goes with it.' In South Wales there were traces of a similar non-feudal philosophy, although already by the middle years of the nineteenth century there were signs of a greater stress there on the solidarity of the new work-force, in time to be a solidarity of socialism, than on the virtues of individualism. There would have been more support there for the qualifying conclusion of Telford's statement – 'but I hold that the aim and end of all ought not to be a mere bag of money, but something far higher and far better.'

In Glasgow, Scotland had provided the great commercial city, just as in Adam Smith it had provided the great political economist who traced the courses of the wealth of nations. Already in 1760 the Carron Iron Works, 'the most extensive manufactory in Europe', had been founded. In 1801 Robert Mushet discovered the black-band ore deposits of the west, and in 1828 J.B. Neilson, manager of a Glasgow gasworks, invented the hot-blast process. Industrial Lanarkshire was only one of Scotland's textile centres. And above all, Scotland produced engineers. 'The work of James Watt,' wrote the author of *Glasgow: its Municipal Organization and Administration* in 1896, 'how mean it would be to say it benefited Glasgow. It revolutionized the world.' The list of Scots engineers is a formidable one, and many of them achieved their greatest triumphs outside Scotland.

In North Wales, there had been an early industrial revolution in the eighteenth century, well described by Professor A.H. Dodd (1951), before the great industrial expansion in South Wales in the nineteenth century.

The village of Bersham, one of the first places where coke iron was made, vied with the Midland ironworks in turning out cannon in the 1760's and cylinders for Watt's steam engine in the '70's. In the '80's Anglesey almost dominated the world market for copper ore, and Holywell was formidable enough for its brass works to arouse the jealous suspicion of Boulton, and its cotton mills that of the Arkwrights. Even after the turn of the century, we find at Llangollen one of the earliest power looms to be successfully worked south of the Tweed, and mills in Montgomeryshire that still carried on a precarious rivalry with the North of England in one branch of the woollen industry.

Thomas Telford's masterpiece, the Menai Straits suspension bridge, completed in 1826.

The great tubular bridges built by Robert Stephenson across the Conway River and the Menai Straits were not completed until 1850 (see below, p. 166). And by then the main industrial development in Wales was unmistakably in the south (Telford's suspension bridge had been built across the straits in an earlier phase during the years 1819 to 1826). South Welsh development, indeed, had been lively even during the eighteenth century, with capital from outside flowing into the area. Anthony Bacon, a London contractor and merchant, set up the Cyfartha Works of Merthyr Tydfil in 1765: his partner was Richard Crawshay, another London contractor and merchant from a similar background. The great Dowlais works of Sir John Guest depended on eight furnaces in 1823 when no Staffordshire furnace had more than four. The Dowlais figure had risen to eighteen by 1846.

Merthyr Tydfil was as characteristic an industrial town as any of the English towns of the same period. At the 1801 Census it had only 7,000 inhabitants, but this was already large by comparison with other places in South Wales. By 1831 the population had risen to 30,000. New immigrants were drawn in, not, as Professor Glanmor Williams has insisted, driven out from their villages. Yet it was an unhappy place, densely crowded and in places extremely unhealthy. J.L. and Barbara Hammond singled it out when they were discussing conditions of life in the 'bleak age' – they quoted a writer of 1848 who, after remarking how clean the interiors of houses in Merthyr Tydfil were, went on:

> The footways are seldom flagged, the streets are ill-paved and with bad materials, and are not lighted. The drainage is very imperfect; there are few underground sewers, no house drains, and the open gutters are not regularly cleaned out. Dust bins and similar receptacles for filth are unknown; the refuse is thrown into the streets. Bombay itself, reputed to be the filthiest town under British sway, is scarcely worse.

No account of locational changes brought about by the industrial revolution would be complete if it did not include a note on what was

113

119

A cartoon, captioned 'Britannia rules the waves!' and published in the American magazine *Puck*, pointed to the possibility that the construction of a Channel Tunnel might not result in friendly co-operation between France and England.

projected and *not* achieved. For every successful building completed – including factories and bridges – there was one which was rejected (either at the design stage or for financial reasons). Thus at Coalbrookdale, when a railway was needed in the 1790s from the New Work Collieries to Horsehay, the finances of the Company were too strained to allow it.

In general, transport was most vulnerable. It is difficult in reading Phillips's book on canals to separate planned from completed projects, and it has been estimated that less than half the railways projected by 1851 had actually been built. There was an enormous amount of talk about a Channel Tunnel – and much imagination and energy was applied to the idea – but no tunnel was built. Nor was a railway link ever constructed across London to join termini linked with the North and the South, as J.R. Kellett has explained in his fascinating, detailed study of *The Impact of Railways on Victorian Cities* (1969). There were too many interests in the way. London schemes were often held up at a time when change in the provincial cities seemed both more practicable and more profitable. And no private enterprise could ever have built James Silk Buckingham's Model Town Victoria (1849), a project using huge quantities of iron and intended to be constructed on a radial plan with factories on the periphery and public buildings at the centre.

Alongside the sites proposed or projected and never developed it is necessary in 1979 to set the industrial and related sites, some of them of the greatest possible interest, which have been destroyed. The catalogue would be far larger than that produced of historic houses by the Victoria and Albert Museum (*The Destruction of the Country House*, 1974). The researches of Peter Reid showed that at least 712 notable country houses in Britain had been demolished, gutted or allowed to fall into ruins since 1945; and certainly during the same period many great industrial landmarks were lost – the railway works at Crewe; the Viaduct of Crumlin; the pumping station of Elkesley (after a public inquiry); the Coal Exchange in the City of London; and, most potent perhaps of all the

92

symbols, the Euston Arch (1962). We are now left not with a fully representative record of the industrial revolution or one which catches the full flavour of it, but with what Anthony Burton rightly calls 'the remains'.

Interest, however, is increasing – for reasons described above in the Prologue. It grows not only in obviously industrial settings, like Ironbridge or the West Riding, but in counties which are not usually associated with industry in the public mind – or in the mind of tourists. Thus Professor Walter Minchinton has produced the delightful guide to *Industrial Archaeology in Devon* (1968).

Below are listed the numbers of visitors in 1977 to some of the surviving industrial sites and buildings. The list followed a pioneering survey made in 1975 for the English Tourist Board by Industrial Market Research Ltd on the North of England Open Air Museum at Beamish; and is published by SAVE Britain's Heritage and included in Marcus Binney and Max Hanna's *Preservation Pays*.

	Ironbridge Open Air Museum: 168,000
NORTH-EAST	Beamish Open Air Museum: 208,000
	Monkwearmouth Station Museum: 74,981
YORKSHIRE	Abbeydale Industrial Hamlet: 64,440
	Bradford Industrial Museum: 89,965
	Hull Town Docks Museum: 69,985
	Hull Transport and Archaeology Museum: 49,778
	Keighley and Worth Valley Light Railway: 149,859
	National Railway Museum, York: 1,440,410
	North Yorkshire Moors Railway: 250,000
SOUTH-EAST	Kent and East Sussex Railway: 37,360
	Tyrwhitt Drake Museum of Carriages: 36,000
EAST ANGLIA	Bressingham Steam Engine Museum: 120,707
	North Norfolk Railway: 90,000
OTHER AREAS	Great Western Society Railway Museum, Didcot: 44,000
	Shuttleworth Collection, Padiham, Lancs: 130,000
	Nottingham Industrial Museum: 354,514
	Great Central Railway, Loughborough: 45,000
	Waterways Museum, Northants: 70,435
	Acton Scott Working Farm Museum: 31,806
	Arlington Hill Museum, Bibury: 52,000
	Gladstone Pottery Museum: 60,000
	Severn Valley Railway: 140,000

All these are interesting places, open to the public, where tourists are gathering. The most exciting way to study the places of the industrial revolution, however, is to explore the forgotten and the remote – even to discover. There are parts of the country where the industrial frontier has receded and nature has taken over again.

Canals as vital arteries

55, 56 Until the arrival of the railways in Britain, inland waterways were vital to the transporting of heavy loads over long distances. The double lock on the Regent's Canal, with the east entrance to the Islington Tunnel in the background, illustrates one type of engineering; the Pont Cysyllte Aqueduct ($3\frac{1}{2}$ miles east of Llangollen), carrying the Ellesmere Canal in a cast-iron trough across the Dee Valley, was a successful answer to the kind of challenge which engineers such as Thomas Telford overcame.

57 The principle of the inclined plane (such as the Hay Incline at Coalbrookdale), used to transfer loads in flat-bottomed boats from one canal (or river) to another at a different level, was shown in a series of engravings published in 1800; the incline was provided with rails and winding gear, and was an essential feature in the efficient working of the inland waterway system.

58, 59 *Opposite*. Examples of the development of canals in continental Europe and North America: the Ludwig Canal (linking Rivers Rhine and Main with the Danube) at Erlangen, in an engraving published in 1845; and the flight of locks at the junction of the Erie and Northern Canals – vital for the economic integration of the Great Lakes region and the eastern seaboard – seen in a coloured aquatint by John Hill, *c.* 1830–2.

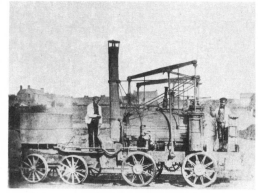

Early railways 60–62 The novel attraction of the railway as a means of passenger transport was exploited by Richard Trevithick in 1809 at Euston Square – for a shilling a ride; a further sixteen years were to elapse before the first commercial passenger service, the Stockton and Darlington line in Co. Durham, was opened in 1825 amid much popular interest and enthusiasm (below). In the struggle to build an efficient locomotive George Stephenson's design proved superior in the end to that of William Hedley, one of whose colliery locomotives – the *Puffing Billy* (above, right) – of 1813 is shown (after reconstruction) in a photograph taken *c.* 1860.

63, 64 Two inaugural events: the opening of Scotland's first passenger service, the Glasgow to Garnkirk line, in 1831; and the Shoreham branch of the London, Brighton and South Coast Railway in 1840 (note the deep cutting through the chalk ridge of the South Downs).

Railway engineering in town and country

65, 66 The rapid spread of the railway system produced many challenges for the engineers. The high-level bridge (which carries both rail and road transport), at Newcastle-upon-Tyne was designed by Robert Stephenson and John Dobson and completed in 1849; (below, left) the magnificently proportioned west entrance to the Box Tunnel on the Great Western Railway near Bath.

67 Engineers sometimes produced elaborate three-tier arrangements for the underground system, railways and roads. This engraving showing a train outside the Clerkenwell Tunnel in East London.

68 The Lickey Incline on the Birmingham and Gloucester Railway: in this lithograph published in 1840, an imported Norris locomotive (from Philadelphia) is shown ascending the bank.

69 *Right.* A proposed scheme for the London Grand Junction Railway included an arched viaduct cutting a swathe through the urban surroundings. The terminus shown had none of the buildings usually associated with railway stations (another plan was approved in 1833).

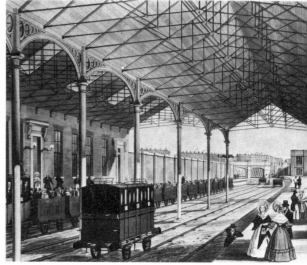

Above

70, 71 The Euston Arch (completed in 1838), with its Doric columns, was built as the monumental entrance to the London and Birmingham Railway's terminus. The interior of the station, by contrast, was purely functional.

72 The London terminus of the Great Northern Railway, King's Cross, was opened in 1852, a year after the main line to Doncaster was completed; this contemporary illustration suggests the atmosphere of bustling activity associated with travel by train from the earliest days.

73 When the railway first came to York the original station stood within the ancient city walls, but with the increase in traffic and the introduction of through services a new, larger station was required. The impressive curved canopy of iron and glass, designed by William Peachy, dates from 1877; it is seen here in a photograph taken shortly after its completion.

74 Like the railways, the London underground system originated with lines operated by private companies: the Metropolitan Railway, from Moorgate to Paddington and beyond, operated mixed-gauge working until *c.* 1850.

75 The first German passenger
service – from Nuremberg to
Fürth – opened in 1835, ten
years after the Stockton and
Darlington line (*ill. 62*), but
with equal popular interest, as
this anonymous watercolour
shows.

76 In the second half of the
nineteenth century, railway
development on the American
continent proceeded apace. An
oil-painting by Juan Gryalva,
c. 1880 (right), gives some idea
of the problems presented by
the hilly terrain in Ecuador,
where the Guayaquil and Quito
Railway follows the contours of
the valley.

77–79 In North America, trains belonging to the Central Pacific and Union Pacific Railroads met at Promontory Point, Utah, on 10 May 1869 amid great rejoicing: west and east coasts were now joined by rail (top). For the traveller, however, there were marked contrasts between the comforts of ordinary travel by the 'ship of the plains', as depicted in *Harper's Weekly* in 1886, and the amenities provided in a Pullman Company parlour car, seen in an engraving published in 1888.

Iron ships and steam propulsion

80–82 Among the various experimental canal- and river-boats tested in Britain, France and America in the 1780s, the *John Fitch* – seen here on the Delaware River at Philadelphia – was propelled by a system of steam-driven paddles. In Scotland in 1802, the famous paddle-tug *Charlotte Dundas* (below, left) proved her worth on the Forth–Clyde Canal, and twenty years later the *Aaron Manby* (below, right) was the first steamboat to cross the English Channel in the course of a journey from London to Paris.

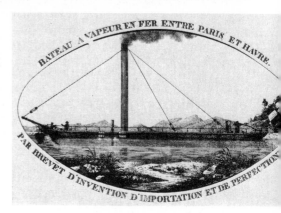

83–85 Two famous examples of iron-hulled ships were Brunel's *Great Britain*, launched at Bristol in July 1843 (left), and the *Great Eastern*, launched in 1859. The latter, giant vessel is chiefly remembered for her role in the laying of the first transatlantic cable, the loading of which is shown here. The *Great Britain*, which made her maiden voyage from Liverpool to New York in 1845, had a varied career – and was finally driven aground in the Falkland Islands in 1886. Today, the restored ship is preserved in dry dock at Bristol.

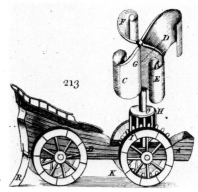

Fanciful and unfulfilled ideas

86, 87 Early ideas for pleasure-garden and personal transport included a man-powered monorail system (advertised in London as an attraction at the Royal Panarmonion Gardens, King's Cross), and a wind-powered vehicle (illustrated in W. Emerson's *The Principles of Mechanics*, 1758) in which the vertically mounted propeller provided direct power, by a system of cogs, to the front wheels.

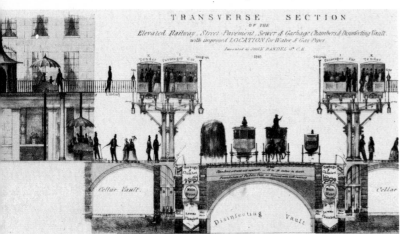

88 An integrated traffic and sewerage scheme for the City of New York, planned in 1848 by the engineer John Randel, was illustrated with impressions of its likely appearance, in this example a cross-section of Broadway; in the 1870s the elevated railway included here became a reality (cf. *ill. 194*).

89 The atmospheric railway depended on the creation of a vacuum in a cast-iron tube with a flanged opening at the top; the South Devon Railway – seen here at Dawlish – abandoned its experiment in 1848 after it had become clear that no satisfactory method of sealing the vacuum could be devised.

90 Among the designs proposed for
the rebuilding of London Bridge was
this one by Thomas Telford,
comprising a single shallow arch in
cast iron. Rennie's more conventional
multi-arch stone structure of 1831 was
dismantled in the 1960s and rebuilt in
the Arizona desert.

91, 92 The English Channel has
always presented a challenge to
engineers: shown here are a detail of a
design for a rail bridge proposed in the
1860s by Thomé de Gamond, and an
idea published in 1851 by Hector
Horeau for a 21-mile submarine
railway tunnel of cast-iron sections –
with the position of the tunnel marked
by lighthouses and beacons.

93, 94 The arrival of the railway led inevitably to the fearful prospect of serious accidents – the well-known fate of William Huskisson on the day the Liverpool and Manchester line opened in 1830 being perhaps an omen for the future. Sir John Tenniel's pencil drawing (left) has a certain macabre quality, but the graphic treatment of an accident on the North London Railway at Kentish Town in September 1861 leaves no doubt about the realities of such disasters.

Opposite
95 'The Touring Season', a poster advertising insurance cover for railway passengers; chromolithograph, 1846.

THE TOURING SEASON

ACCIDENTS BY RAIL, ROAD, RIVER OR SEA

When Travelling, boating, walking, riding, cricketing, cycling &c.

Insured against by the

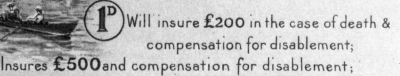

RAILWAY PASSENGERS ASSURANCE CO

ESTABLISHED 1849.

TOURISTS & the Public generally can Assure against

ALL ACCIDENTS
By Annual or Short term Policy.

CONVEYANCE ACCIDENTS
By Policies for one or three months.

RAILWAY ACCIDENTS
By Annual Policies or by Tickets for the Tourists :-

1ᴰ Will insure £200 in the case of death & compensation for disablement;

2ᴰ Insures £500 and compensation for disablement;

3ᴰ Insures £1,000, £6 weekly for total & £1·10 weekly for Partial disablement.

WHEN BOOKING ASK FOR INSURANCE TICKET.

For further particulars see other side, and apply to Agents at Railway Stations in all Towns or to — A. VIAN sec.

64, CORNHILL, LONDON.

96 A romantic view of James Watt observing the
condensation of steam is provided in this mezzotint by
James Scott after Marcus Stone, 1869. Watt's
discovery and his practical application of it in the low-
pressure steam-engine with a separate condenser were
among the most significant advances in the use of
steam as a source of power.

SUMMING UP the effects of the industrial revolution on the map of England, the geographer Professor W. G. East concluded that 'industrial capitalism, when it matured, produced changes on the map which were, perhaps, unequalled in magnitude by any others subsequent to the Anglo-Saxon settlement'.

'Industrial capitalism' is not an abstraction, however, and the term had not yet come into use in the period covered in this book. There could have been no initiating, let alone maturing, without the drive and effort of particular people, individuals and groups. Indeed, just as it is possible to trace the development of industrialization in terms of places and their relationships with each other, so it is possible to trace it in terms of people and their relationships.

A few of them are well-remembered people, outstanding inventors, engineers and businessmen. The alphabet starts inevitably with 'A for Arkwright', described by the first Sir Robert Peel as 'a man who has done more honour to the country than any man I know, not excepting our great military characters', and ends with Watt, Wedgwood and Wilkinson:

> Engine of Watt! unrivall'd is thy sway.
> Compared with thine, what is the tyrant's power?
> His might destroys, while thine creates and saves.

Watt was invited by one 'tyrant', Catherine the Great of Russia, to become 'Master Founder of Iron Ordnance to her Imperial Majesty' but respectfully declined. Watt was not knighted, however; Arkwright was.

Large numbers of inventors, engineers and businessmen who made significant contributions to technical and economic development – the patent records bear witness to them – are far less well known generally by name, and even more have left no names behind them. The French economist, J. B. Say, was right in 1826 (see above, p. 39) to point both to enterprise and to execution. Inventors and businessmen between them transformed the sense of enterprise, considering their most valuable assets to be not business stocks but working machines. Yet enterprise, however striking, was always only one element in the story. There could have been no industrial revolution without the new 'labour force', as political economists came to call it, or the 'working classes' as they came to conceive of themselves during the processes of industrialization.

The changing pattern of skills was an indispensable component. But hard work, too, was equally indispensable in the remaking of the physical environment. The 'navvies' working first on the canals and later on the railways are as important a part of the *dramatis personae* of the industrial revolution as the cotton-spinners. There was, indeed, a remarkably varied labour force or working class. As a perspicacious Leeds minister put it in 1845, 'A coal or an iron field gathers upon it a manufacturing race. No immigration can account for the sudden rise. It is a nidus of a new commonwealth.' R. W. Hamilton did not lament the development. 'A new

3 People

114

Richard Arkwright (1732–92), industrial pioneer; detail of a portrait by Joseph Wright of Derby, c. 1789–90.

Samuel Crompton (1753–1827), inventor of the spinning 'mule', one of the most important new devices introduced into textile manufacturing.

order of men now belongs to us. They are our artificers and operatives. The national character has received new elements into it.'

The 'navvies', often colourful, always distinctive, in their dress, had immense muscular strength and could handle their picks with 'uncommon dexterity'. Anthony Burton has described the men who built the canals (1972) and Terry Coleman the men who built the railways (1965). The latter received more attention than the 'Navigators', who were sometimes treated as *banditti*, 'as completely a class by themselves as the gipsies'. The railway had more friends in high places. 'There comes a crowd of burly navvies, with pickaxes and barrows,' wrote George Eliot, 'and while hardly a wrinkle is made in the feeding mother's face, or a new curve of health in the blooming girl's, the hills are cut through, or the breaches between them spanned, we choose our level, and the white steam-pennon flies along.' Their lives were usually short, however, and they were easy victims of disaster.

From one point of view, however, it was the workers with machines who were the most significant group in the labour force, for the machine production (described more fully in Chapter IV) was a central feature of industrialization. On the eve of the great industrial expansion, Adam Smith had relatively little to say about machines, concentrating more on the division of labour. Yet three years after *The Wealth of Nations* the anonymous author of *Letters on Employing Machines to Shorten Labour* generalized optimistically:

Read the history of mankind, consider the gradual steps of civilization from barbarism to refinement, and you will not fail to discover that the progress of society from its lowest and worst to its highest and most perfect state has been uniformly accompanied and chiefly promoted by the happy exertions of man in the character of a mechanic or an engineer. Let all machines be destroyed, and we are reduced in a moment to the condition of savages; and in that state men may exist a long time without the aid of curious and complex machines; though without them they can never rise above it.

It was almost a commonplace by the mid-nineteenth century that there was a greater distance between 'a savage and the least skilled labourer' than there was between 'that least skilled labourer and the most competent and active manager, inventor and employer.' The Whig *Edinburgh Review*, written and read for the most part by people outside industry, hailed 'progress' and saluted those with very special skills who were contributing towards it: 'The human operative, in imitation and by the aid of the machine, acquires a perfection little less than marvellous. The rapidity of his motion, the acuteness of his perception render him a fitting companion for the intricate mechanism he employs.'

Yet such panegyric, common in the middle years of the nineteenth century and reaching its peak, perhaps, in 1859, the year of the funeral of Robert Stephenson (born 1803), has not been universal. Thirty-five years elapsed, for example, before the town of Bolton erected a statue of Samuel Crompton (the inventor of the famous 'mule'), who had died an unacclaimed and embittered man in 1829. And when nearly half a century later Waterhouse's new Town Hall was built in Manchester, there was no place in its Hall of Sculpture – or for that matter in its impressive wall-paintings by Ford Madox Brown – for the heroes of the industrial revolution. Sir William Fairbairn, the distinguished engineer and author of *Mills and Millwork* (1862), had urged in vain that Arkwright, Watt and the Duke of Bridgewater should be represented. Instead, Fairbairn himself was left to represent them all.

George Stephenson, better known to posterity even than Watt because he is identified not with the steam-engine but with the railway, was perhaps exceptional: 'he seemed', wrote a friend, 'the impersonation of the moving, active spirit of the age'. And certainly the silent crowds lining the streets leading to Westminster Abbey in 1859 for Robert Stephenson's funeral (he was buried next to Telford) were as respectful as they had been some years before at the funeral of the Duke of Wellington. By then – and the moment was a passing one – the nation seemed to be identified with industrial supremacy, as it had been eight years before at the Great Exhibition. Near the beginning of the nineteenth century (1803), *The Gentleman's Magazine* had not bothered to include inventors, industrialists or engineers in a series of lists of distinguished contemporaries which picked out 'Ministers and Statesmen, Lawyers, Judges, Divines, Voyagers, Travellers, Mathematicians and Naturalists'. This marked a retreat from Francis Bacon's seventeenth-century vision of a 'College of Inventors' which would include two galleries for statues of 'Inventors past' and 'spaces or bases for Inventors to come'.

When the lives of engineers came to be written, Samuel Smiles was the most readable. His *George Stephenson* (1864) was a best-seller and he went on writing industrial biographies even when his popularity as an author was waning. Yet he recognized that the engineers should be allowed, when they were articulate enough, to speak for themselves, and he produced an edition in 1883 of the autobiography of James Nasmyth (1808–90), who had settled in Manchester in 1835 and pioneered the machine-tool industry without which the momentum of the process of industrialization could never have been maintained. Nasmyth's name, indeed, needs to be singled out – as does that of Joseph Whitworth (1803–87), who had settled in Manchester two years before him. Whitworth standardized the thread of screws; Nasmyth invented the steam-hammer, and also built 109 railway locomotives in fourteen years.

It is interesting to study even anonymous autobiography. In 1868 'A Civil Engineer' published his *Personal Recollections of English Engineers and of the Introduction of the Railway System into the United Kingdom*, which is a fascinating study of what went on behind the scenes and of the differences between various engineers as people. 'It is the hope of the writer', the anonymous author stated in his Preface, 'that anecdotes of Stephenson and Brunel, of engineering and of railway warfare and advance, and of the revolution effected by the introduction of railways into England, Wales and Ireland will not be less attractive than tales of Ferdinand and of Francis of Naples, of Garibaldi and the English legion, and of the struggle between civilization and the Papacy.'

'A Civil Engineer' was willing to cast his net rather wider than Smiles. 'To select none but meritorious men for portraiture would be an attempt to falsify human nature. It is rather from a contemplation of our past failures, than from that of our partial successes, that we must hope to derive lessons for future improvement.' He was particularly enlightening in the comparison he drew between I. K. Brunel and Robert Stephenson, almost exact contemporaries who died within weeks of each other:

George Stephenson
(1781–1848), railway pioneer;
Stevengraph woven in silk.

VIII

The imperfections of the character of Mr. Brunel were of the heroic order. He saw always clearly before him the thing to be done and the way to do it, although he might be deficient in the choice and the management of the human agency which was necessary to effect his designs. Mr. Stephenson, on the other hand, knew how to derive from his staff and his friends a support and an aid that carried him, at times, over real engineering difficulties with a flowing sheet. It may be that the perfection and success of each individual work was more the study and aim of Mr. Brunel, the return of benefit to the shareholders the more present idea to Mr. Stephenson. The former preferred the luxurious cabins of Atlantic steamers and the commodious sofas of the Broad Gauge carriages: the latter opened the way for parliamentary and workmen's trains.

This is more acute than Smiles, and it is just that the copy of *Personal Recollections* in the library of the Institution of Civil Engineers (to which Telford had bequeathed his books) identifies the author as F. R. Conder, a pupil of Stephenson. Along with Sir Francis Head's *Stokers and Pokers* (1845), *Personal Recollections* captures for all time the immediacy of the period.

Putting together autobiographies, biographies, catalogues, trade and city directories and the like, along with all the ephemera, it is difficult in the twentieth century to get at the people as they really were. L. T. C. Rolt's biographies are an impressive attempt (he has dealt with Newcomen, the Brunels, the Stephensons and Telford) based on original researches, and the whole corpus is illuminated by his own revealing autobiography. There are a few cases where full-length biography has had to wait until the twentieth century. Ian McNeill's *Joseph Bramah* (1968) is a study of perhaps the most versatile of the eighteenth-century engineers (1749–1814; when he died, *The Gentleman's Magazine* printed a glowing obituary, but that was almost the last word). Apart from his own work, Bramah is important because he brings out a pedigree. One of his pupils, Henry Maudslay, played a key role in the development of machine tools, and Maudslay's own pupils included Nasmyth and Whitworth; Richard Roberts (1789–1844), who invented many tools, including a screw-cutting lathe and a hole-puncher for iron (used when workmen building Robert Stephenson's tubular Britannia Bridge across the Menai Straits went on strike); Samuel Seaward (1800–42), who went on to specialize in marine engineering; David Napier (1790–1869) who made printing-machines before turning to armaments; and John Clement, assistant to Charles Babbage (1792–1871), in some ways the most brilliant of all the early pioneers. Babbage's *Economy of Manufactures* (1833) is a classic, and his mechanical computer was less a wonder of the age than a pointer to what might be done when steam had given way to electricity and a new generation of electrical engineers had been born.

What look like individual biographies are linked in time, therefore, through pedigrees, like the Telford pedigree. They are linked also through networks at particular moments of time. Who knew whom? Who wrote to whom? Who hired or fired whom? Who bought from whom? Who were the rivals – and the partners? William Muir, a second cousin of William Murdoch, who had worked with Watt, became Maudslay's draughtsman and co-operated closely with Whitworth. Murdoch, who had built a model locomotive in 1784, had produced gas from coal (1792), which was used to light the Soho Works in 1798, and it was a pupil of his, Samuel Clegg, who helped to build up London's impressive Gas Light and Coke Company, founded in 1812.

Detailed technical history, pioneered by H. W. Dickinson, who delved in many dark places (for example in his life of Boulton), brings out into the open such networks . . . just as industrial archaeology restores sites. Yet it remains difficult to distil generalizations from biographies . . . generalizations about background, motivations and fortunes of the kind which sociologists like. As T. S. Ashton wrote in 1948, when the industrial revolution was just beginning to be reassessed by economic historians, 'it was from no single zone of thrift and enterprise that the trade winds blew.' 'Some of the inventors learnt from the job, their job: there was no important manufacture,' Benjamin Franklin claimed in 1783, in which workmen 'have not invented some useful process, which saves time and materials, or improves the workmanship.' Likewise, some of the workmen became employers themselves: their social mobility depended not only on the degree of their enterprise, but on the capital required to set up on their own and the terms on which it was available.

Many of the textile-manufacturers started modestly, some with a little land, some with a little money, many with neither. At Keighley, Lodge

Francis Darby (1783–1850), ironmaster, was manager of the Coalbrookdale Works from 1810 until his death; oil-painting by L. Corbett.

THE DARBY FAMILY DYNASTY

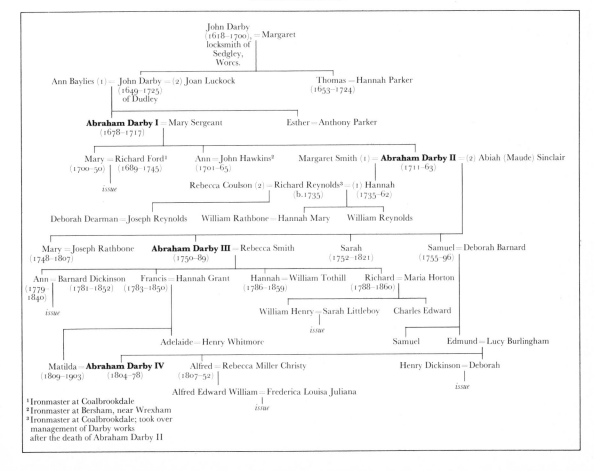

John Smeaton (1724–92), whose notable achievements included the building of the new Eddystone Lighthouse in Plymouth Sound – a stone tower completed in 1759; engraving from Samuel Smiles, *Lives of the Engineers* (1874 ed.).

Calvert was a joiner (he started with a throstle and a miniature spinning-frame turned by hand), Joseph Craven was a stuff piece maker, John Brigg a yeoman farmer, James Smith a grocer. Most of the ironmasters were men who had started in secondary metal trades. Thus Abraham Darby I's father, Henry, was a locksmith, Ambrose Crowley and Richard Crawshay worked in ironmongers' shops, Aaron Walker was a nailer, Peter Stubs of Rotherham a filemaker and Samuel Garbett a brassworker.

Many but not all of the ironmasters were Nonconformists. All the Darbys, of course, were Quakers: intensely concerned, they also married Quakers. The first two placed the control of Coalbrookdale into the hands of Quaker relatives before their children reached maturity. There were 'dynastic' marriages, too, with other families of ironmasters outside Coalbrookdale. The Lloyd family followed a similar pattern, which favoured a certain aloofness from the world, sensible business relations, hard work, frugality, the reinvestment of capital and sometimes, as with the Lloyds, a shift into banking. There were Methodist ironmasters, too, in the late eighteenth century – the Yorkshire Walkers, for instance, John Roebuck and possibly John Wilkinson, were Independents. Matthew Boulton was of a different temperament, steering 'a true course between the ascetic rocks and sensual whirlpools'.

There were a few inventors – and some businessmen, too – who started right outside the growing industrial complex. The best-known case, perhaps, was that of Dr Edmund Cartwright (1793–1823), Rector of Goadby Marwood, near Melton Mowbray in Leicestershire, who – 'never at the time having seen a person weave' – invented a power loom. (After actually seeing a person weave he substantially improved his loom.) 'There was nothing in the pursuits of the first half of his life', his daughter wrote comprehensively, 'calculated to lead his mind to study the theory of mechanics, or in his habits to bring him acquainted with their practical application.' He made no profit out of his invention (compare Arkwright's fortune), though the government made him a grant of £10,000. Even the town where he died, Hastings in Sussex, is outside the industrial area, and he was buried at near-by Battle. He was just as different from James Kay (1704–81), inventor of the flying shuttle (1733), as he was from Arkwright. And Kay's own strange life, which involved attacks on his furniture and his home and ended in exile in France, is difficult to fit into any pattern. It is not even known where *he* is buried.

Kay, the son of a yeoman farmer, was the youngest of twelve children: Arkwright, the son of poor parents, was one of thirteen. Bramah, the son of a coachman to an earl, was one of only four. George Stephenson, son of an engineman at a pit, was the second child of six. How different they all were from Dr John Smeaton (1724–92), elected a Fellow of the Royal Society at the early age of twenty-nine. And how different Smeaton was from the millwright James Brindley (1716–72), whose technical interests were very similar.

If we go back to the alphabet, Arkwright (1732–92) was a barber by trade and had little education. He is said to have moved into textiles because wigs went out of fashion (Boulton had fortunately moved out of buckles long before they went out of fashion). How much he actually invented was always a matter of controversy. At the other end of the alphabet, Samuel Walker, the Yorkshire iron-smelter, was a schoolmaster. In 1741 he built his first furnace in an old nailer's smithy at Rotherham, and four years later he had become so successful that, in his own words, he was 'obliged to give up' his school.

What would Boulton have done without Watt? He had started as a 'toy manufacturer' – 'toys' including everything from bells to buckles – but from 1774 onwards his business was transformed. In that year James Watt (1736–1819), one of the relatively small number of inventors and industrialists who had experienced formal scientific training (at Glasgow University) and had in 1768 invented a steam-engine known as 'Beelzebub' in Scotland, joined Boulton at the Soho Works in Birmingham. (He had worked previously in Scotland with John Roebuck, educated as a doctor, at the Carron Iron Works.)

Industrial personalities as viewed by different colleagues or different rivals looked quite different. Boulton had strong opinions about Arkwright, for example: 'tyranny and an improper exercise of power will not do in this country. . . . If Arkwright had been a more civilized being and understood mankind better, he would now have enjoyed his patent.' Yet Boulton and Watt enjoyed their steam-engine patent for nearly a quarter of a century only in face of opposition, trying with varying degrees of success to prevent other engineers from constructing other types of engine under licence. Watt thought Murdoch's model locomotive no more than a toy, and Richard Trevithick (1771–1833), the Cornish inventor of a real working steam locomotive (patented 1802; built 1803), carried out all his experiments in the face of Watt's bitter disapproval. His high-pressure engine was an immense advance on Watt's low-pressure engine. There was little bitter about Trevithick, who claimed later in his life that on visits to the North-East he had often dandled the young Robert Stephenson on his knee.

George Hudson (1800–71), the financier and 'railway king', whose career ended prematurely in disgrace.

The Stephensons both had their own share of bitter attack. When Dr Dionysius Lardner eulogized George as 'the father of the locomotive' in a lecture at Newcastle in 1836, William Hedley inserted a notice in the local newspapers for three weeks claiming he had fathered it first. In the last years of his life George thought that there were too many railways. 'What a Railway World this is. When will the bustle be over?' He had been a friend of George Hudson (1800–71), 'the railway king', who as projector and speculator was at the heart of all the bustle ('Mak' all t' railways come to York', he is said to have urged.) Hudson's career collapsed in ruins in 1849 and the 'mania' ended, but George, who had by then died, had foreseen the dangers. 'Hudson has become too great a man for me now. . . . I have made Hudson a rich man, but he will very soon care for nobody except he can get money from them.'

Hudson, whom Gladstone once hailed as 'a projector of great discernment, courage and rich enterprise', was looking for victims, not partners. Without partnerships between people of complementary qualities (or resources), however, there could have been no industrial revolution. The company form of industrial organization had not yet fully developed: the canals and railways did much to hasten it. Nor was there limited liability. Trust in people was essential for success in business. Names may have been forgotten subsequently, but there could be no anonymity at the time.

Boulton and Watt formed a classic partnership, one of the many, which characterized the industrial revolution. Another formative partnership was that between Arkwright and Jedediah Strutt (1726–97), a hosiery-

Marc Isambard Brunel
(1769–1849) and Isambard
Kingdom Brunel (1806–59),
who formed a remarkable
father-and-son pair in the world
of engineering.

manufacturer: together they established a mill at Nottingham, moving to Cromford in 1771. Arkwright in turn lent money to Samuel Oldknow (1756–1828). Both these associations are well documented. An Oldknow document of 1786 (from his London agents) is particularly memorable: 'You have many competitors, we know, coming forward. . . . You must give a look to Invention, Industry you have in abundance. . . . We expect to hear from you as soon as possible and as the sun shines let us make the hay.' As for Strutt, he wrote his own obituary: 'Here rests in peace J.S. – Who, without Fortune, Family or Friends raised himself a Fortune, Family and Name in the World – Without having wit had a good share of plain Common Sense – without much genius enjoyed the more substantial blessing of a Sound understanding.'

A very different kind of association from that between Arkwright and Strutt was that between the second Duke of Bridgewater (1736–1803) and the unlettered millwright James Brindley. Brindley, 'the greatest enthusiast in favour of artificial navigations that ever existed', designed the Bridgewater Canal: the Duke more than anyone else admired his 'all-contriving power . . . to encounter all difficulties and to remove the most perplexing obstacles'. And after the Canal was completed he joined Josiah Wedgwood (1730–95) and others in promoting the Grand Trunk Canal, again with Brindley as designer and implementor (although the Canal was not completed until five years after his death). 'Gentlemen came to view our eighth wonder of the world,' wrote an anonymous pamphleteer, 'the subterranean navigation, which is cutting by the great Mr. Brindley, who handles rocks as easily as you would plum pies and makes the four elements subservient to his will.' Similar remarks were to be made in grander fashion (and in verse as well as in prose) by Southey about Telford, who himself had started his career as an apprentice to the mason of the Duke of Buccleuch. Bridgewater was by no means the only member of the aristocracy to interest himself in or derive large profits from trade and industry. Mining was one lucrative source, and there were other connections too.

Brindley built a flint mill for Wedgwood at Leek, and it was Wedgwood who said of him on his death that his works would be 'the most lasting monument to his time' and would 'show to future ages how much good may be done by one single genius, when happily employed upon works beneficial to Mankind.' That is how civil engineers thought of themselves. The word 'civil' was first used in contrast to 'military' or 'naval', but by the beginning of the nineteenth century it had a ring of its own: the Institution of Civil Engineers, founded in 1818, captured it. Brindley himself left no records and undertook his ambitious projects without preparing elaborate drawings or calculations, but many of the civil engineers, like Telford, were as adept at producing reports or drawing blueprints as they were at construction itself. 'Civil engineers are a self-created set of men,' Smeaton said with pride, 'whose profession owes its origin, not to power or influence, but to the best of all protection, the encouragement of a great and powerful nation.'

There was no great dividing line, however, between civil and mechanical engineers, and it was not until 1847, when the civil engineers had acquired immense prestige, that the Institution of Mechanical Engineers was created. Brindley patented an improvement of Newcomen's steam-engine, for example, and John Rennie, a former student at Edinburgh University, built a bridge before he planned the machinery for Boulton and Watt's Albion Mills: he used wheels of wrought and cast iron in place of wood. In 1798 he redesigned a new Royal Mint. Rennie was the father of an equally famous engineering son, Sir John Rennie. Apart from the Rennies and the Stephensons, there was one other remarkable father-son pair – Marc Isambard Brunel (1769–1849), who was born in France, lived and worked for six years in the United States (where he designed a gun-foundry and submitted a winning design for a new Congress Building in Washington which was never built), and arrived in London in 1799, and Isambard Kingdom Brunel (1806–59). It was of the son that *The Engineer* wrote long after his death – 'In all that constitutes an engineer in the highest, fullest and best sense, Brunel had no contemporary, no predecessor.' His achievement – the building of the Great Western Railway, with its broad gauge and its great viaducts (58 miles of railway a year for eighteen years), of the Clifton Suspension Bridge at Bristol, and of the first transatlantic steamships ('terminus New York'), culminating in the *Great Eastern* – was on an epic scale, with tragedy at the end, for the *Great Eastern* venture was responsible for his financial ruin and premature death. The father, too, was a masterful figure, and to one contemporary, who knew them both, he 'far excelled' the son 'in originality, unworldliness, genius and taste'. In a recent biography (1970) Paul Clements has described his long life, which also reached an epic culmination – the construction of the first tunnel under the Thames – the first tunnel anywhere in the world beneath the soft bed of a river.

John Rennie (1761–1821), engineer and bridge-builder; engraving from Samuel Smiles, *Lives of the Engineers* (1874 ed.).

The exploits of the engineers make for superb biography. Yet an industrialist involved in a very different range of enterprises, Josiah Wedgwood, is one of the most interesting and attractive personalities of the industrial revolution, with his strong opinions about changing consumer needs (and the opportunities they offered him) on the one side, and about 'tasteful' art and design (he employed men like John Flaxman to produce his 'ornamental' patterns) on the other. He was a man who loved to experiment, and he was elected a Fellow of the Royal Society in 1783. Beginning in humble circumstances, he later 'converted a rude and inconsiderable manufactory into an elegant art and important element in national commerce'. Simeon Shaw, in his *History of the Staffordshire Potteries* (1829), stressed his industry and perseverance. 'There was room for such a person in a manufacture gradually rising into eminence. Britain was now destined to behold him render the manufacture of pottery celebrated in a degree it had never previously acquired.'

Wedgwood, like Arkwright, is said to have left a fortune of £500,000, and he founded a dynasty which in the nineteenth and twentieth centuries was to inter-marry with some of the country's outstanding intellectual families, including the Darwins. The Darby dynasty had fewer connections and retained its Quaker outlook. Some early industrial pioneers left no family at all.

Josiah Wedgwood (1730–95), the famous Staffordshire pottery-manufacturer and entrepeneur; portrait in oils by Sir Joshua Reynolds.

In the light of this survey of connections, networks and pedigrees, it is misleading to think of the first industrialists as unqualified individualists, pursuing their own interests or those of their families. As Professor T.S. Ashton has written, 'in the eighteenth century the characteristic instrument of social purpose was not the individual or the state, but the Club . . . every interest, tradition or aspiration found expression in corporate form.'

Manchester manufacturers, new though their cotton industry was, gathered together in the eighteenth century whenever they felt that their interests were at stake. Thus, in 1774 they convened a general meeting at Crompton's Coffee House 'to consider proper measures for the security and encouragement of the cotton, linen and other manufactures of this Town and Neighbourhood'. They went on to appoint a Committee with a Chairman, Treasurer and Secretary. There were similar committees, too, in Leeds, Halifax, Exeter and Birmingham (1783).

Ironmasters were even more renowned for frequently combining together for both private and public purposes. Thus, as early as 1762, Abraham Darby II entered into an agreement with Isaac and John Wilkinson to charge a uniform price for cylinders, pipes and other articles in markets other than London. Thus, during the 1770s, William Gibbons of Bristol wrote to the Birmingham ironmasters to suggest resisting in common any imports of iron from the colonies.

During the 1780s the ironmasters (and Matthew Boulton and James Watt) played an important part in the creation of the General Chamber of the Manufacturers of Great Britain. Wedgwood provided the initial stimulus, and many cotton men joined in, too. 'It seems hitherto to have escaped the notice of the manufacturers', the First Plan for the Chamber stated, 'that whilst the *landed* and the *funded interests* . . . have their respective advocates in the great council of the nation, *they* alone are destitute of that advantage.' The Birmingham Committee went further, indeed, and resolved in 1786 that 'the present conjunction of affairs peculiarly demands the firm union, the serious attention, and the vigorous and judicious exertions of the whole body of British manufacturers.' There were differences of opinion and interest, however, among a rather disparate group, and, following a dispute about trade and tariffs, the Chamber soon broke up.

There were differences of opinion later also. Manchester was divided politically in the 1790s at the time of the trial of Thomas Walker, the Unitarian manufacturer, who had been active in the days of the Chamber and was a supporter of the French Revolution, even though a new Commercial Society was formed with enthusiasm in 1794. And there were differences of outlook among manufacturers there at the end of the Napoleonic Wars and even in the heyday of the Anti-Corn Law League, a remarkably well-organized pressure group, in the 1840s. The Manchester Chamber of Commerce was created in 1820, however, and remained active – if rather sporadically – whatever the vicissitudes of trade and politics. Birmingham had set up a new Commercial Committee – after many quarrels in an older Committee – seven years earlier, but it was not until 1819 that the term 'Chamber of Manufactures and Commerce' was employed, and the Chamber lapsed between 1832 and 1842: its records do not start until 1855. By then Leeds had a Chamber (1851), as did Liverpool (1850). There were then said to be twenty Chambers in existence, and the mover of the resolution proposing one in Leeds stressed 'the practical advantages [which] have accrued to commerce and manufactures in those parts of the country where they have been formed'.

'It is the right of every subject', the Manchester cotton-spinners proclaimed in 1800, 'to dispose of his stock and industry where and in what manner he thinks proper.' 'To restrain the spinner in the free disposition of the produce of his manufactory . . . is a violation of his rights and an infringement upon the freedom of trade.' The existence of clubs and associations qualified such ideologies, although the ideologies became more popular after 1813, first in the struggle against the Corn Laws and second in the fight against State intervention in relation to the hours and conditions of work.

Meanwhile, groups offering communication among equals or proclaiming an interest in professional standards were just as influential as the kind of interest groups which had been the object of Adam Smith's attention on the eve of the industrial revolution. Smeaton's Society of Civil Engineers met in London at the King's Head Tavern in Holborn in 1771, seventeen years after the founding by William Shipley of the Society for the Encouragement of Arts, Commerce and Manufactures. Its first President, Thomas Yeoman, had been employed for thirty years in draining the Fens, and it provided ample opportunities for combining conviviality and science. So, too, did the Derby Philosophical Society, established in 1784, with Erasmus Darwin as its first President .

The most famous of all such societies was the Lunar Society of Birmingham, which brought together in the 1770s and 1780s a group of men from outside as well as inside Birmingham who all played key roles in Britain's industrialization – among them (in strict alphabetical order) Matthew Boulton, Erasmus Darwin, Joseph Priestley, James Watt and Josiah Wedgwood. They met for dinner and informal discussion at a member's house once a month in the afternoon of the Monday nearest the time of the full moon (the intention being to take maximum advantage of the moonlight for their journeys home after the meeting), this being the basis of their Society's name. Boulton, like Wedgwood, was a member not only of this Society but of Smeaton's Society of Civil Engineers and the Society for the Encouragement of Arts, Commerce and Manufactures. Another influential member was Benjamin Franklin's friend, Dr William Small, who had spent several years in Virginia.

In Manchester the Literary and Philosophical Society, a lively expression of provincial culture, had James Watt jun. as a member, and the author of its first volume of memoirs (1785) stated proudly that 'the numerous Societies, for the promotion of Literature and Philosophy, which have been formed in different parts of Europe, in the course of the last and present centuries, have been not only the means of diffusing knowledge more extensively, but have contributed to produce a greater number of important discoveries, than have been effected in any other equal space of time.'

The workers had 'clubs', too, not only in well-established crafts like printing but in textiles, and they, too, were capable of discussing ideas as well as of actively promoting their interests. There were sick clubs, too, and clubs like the Friendly Associated Cotton Spinners of Manchester and Stockport which tried to provide insurance against unemployment. The numbers of 'associations' of various kinds grew significantly after the first generation of industrial experience. The idea of 'union' was particularly *XI* strong among working men – as it was among many employers – during the 1820s and 1830s, with the future Chartist, William Lovett, an independent craftsman of a type familiar before the industrial revolution, advocating in 1829 'joint-stock associations of labour' which would ultimately 'have the trade, manufactures and commerce of the country in their own hands'.

The economic and social advantages of 'association' were stressed also. In an age of low wages (though industrial workers' wages were significantly higher than earnings in agriculture) and of social insecurity (economic fluctuations were described tellingly as 'convulsions' and the State did little to mitigate them), 'association' or 'co-operation' was canvassed as offering protection against poverty, providing benefits in times of contingency, and, above all, of expressing 'independence'. In 1848 Christopher Thomson, in his *Autobiography of an Artisan*, described 'association' as 'the very feature of this age'.

There had, of course, been an alternative strand in working-class history. Hargreaves had his home attacked, his windows broken and his furniture destroyed; and Arkwright's factories at Nottingham and Chorley were burnt down. And during and following the Napoleonic Wars groups of handloom weavers in the West Riding combined to threaten to destroy mills if power looms were not removed. Charlotte Brontë's *Shirley* (1849), written after the event, was one of the relatively few industrial novels to take up such themes; and when it appeared, Chartism, a movement of accumulated discontent, maintained, often uneasily, the unifying slogan 'peacefully if we may, forcibly if we must'.

Early industrial society, therefore, was a divided society, and the divisions were apparent both in the workplace and in the 'community'. Employers might flee from the town or city into the countryside: the 'operatives' had to stay at their machines, 'which knew no weariness', and in the streets. Religion could bridge some of the gulfs and there was a strong sense of attachment to the local place. Yet it took time for new ways of work and of life to become routines, and for new institutions (like the trade union) and amenities (like the public park) to emerge. Some of the first people to popularize the term 'industrial revolution', like Arnold Toynbee in the 1880s, emphasized the contrasts more than the general transformation. 'Side by side with a great increase of wealth was seen an enormous increase of pauperism; and production on a vast scale, the result of free competition, had led to a rapid alienation of classes and the degradation of a large body of producers.' The conclusion, a prelude to the late-twentieth-century debate on the standard of living during early industrialization, was simple – 'free competition may produce wealth without producing well-being'.

There is more to be said about the emergence of a new type of more independent working man – something very different from a pauper – and of a new working class confident of its future if not of its present. The integration of a larger element of the population – a rapidly expanding population – in the factory system was compatible, however, with continuing, even strengthened, paternalism as well as with direct action; and there were not only many 'respectful' and respectable' working men but an 'aristocracy of labour' and many grades of intermediate workers both in the textiles industry (overlookers) and in the metal industries (factors) who 'linked' 'masters' and 'men'.

There were a few individuals, too, who belong both to the history of enterprise and to labour history. The most prominent of them was Robert Owen (1771–1858), who moved from Manchester to New Lanark as a manufacturer and produced some of the best yarn in the country. New Lanark was a testing-place for Owen's theory that 'if the care as to the state of your inanimate machines can produce such beneficial results, what may not be expected if you devote equal attention to your vital machines, which are far more wonderfully constructed.' Owen went on to elaborate a theory of co-operation instead of competition. He never fully accepted the existence of 'class', but he won large numbers of working-class adherents among people who did. They were proud of their labour and believed that they were entitled to rewards which would cover the full value of it.

Marx reacted against 'utopian' socialism, as he called it, of the Owenite variety, and he looked ahead to the 'contradictions' inherent in capitalism causing its overthrow. He saw, too, that one of the tendencies of machine production was for the machines to be considered more important than the men: in this connection he often quoted one of his favourite whipping-boys, Dr Andrew Ure, who had in his *Philosophy of Manufactures* argued that 'the most perfect manufacture is that which dispenses entirely with manual labour'.

The implications of such statements are considered more fully in the chapter on 'processes' which follows. Meanwhile, however, the fact that leading sectors of the new industrial system, not only the textiles industries and coal-mining, relied heavily on the labour of children and of women during the early stages of industrialization, reinforced many hostile images of industry. In 1814 George Walker, the Leeds artist, in his description of factory-workers, complained as Owen did, that 'progress' was too frequently being bought at the expense of both health and morals.

> The little blue dirty group in the Plate [of Yorkshire mill-workers] are painted in their true colours; but where in their complexions would the painter discover the blooming carnations of youth, or the valetudinarian, in the surrounding scenery, the pure air necessary for health? Many proprietors of factories have, much to their credit, remedied these evils by a strict attention to the morals, behaviour, and cleanliness of the children, and by adopting the very easy and effective plan of consuming or burning the smoke.

Owen was less sanguine:

> We are unacquainted with any nation, ancient or modern, that has suffered its hundreds of thousands of children of seven to twelve years of age to work incessantly for fifteen hours per day in an overheated, unhealthy atmosphere, allowing them only forty minutes out of that time for dinner and change of air, which they breathe often in damp cellars or in garrets, in confined narrow streets or dirty lanes.

By the time of the Great Exhibition, which put the spotlight on the workers in industry, the bees in the hive, the first restriction of working hours – the Ten Hours Act of 1847 – had been passed after protracted struggles (it dealt with the textiles industry only), as had the first national Public Health Act, a year later. The State was being drawn increasingly into the procedures of social control. Neither the inventors nor the industrialists were to be left completely free, as they had been hitherto, to fashion a new society.

There were, indeed, strident and conflicting voices in the new society. The industrialists themselves had used political pressure to secure the repeal of the Corn Laws in 1846 – W. Cooke Taylor, in his influential *Notes of a Tour in the Manufacturing Districts* (1832), thought that politics was giving the employers 'form' and 'cohesion' – and the Chartists had already

Opposite
97 The strong ties of family life among the British working classes in Victorian times are suggested in this engraving – 'Myself? Or the Children?' – accompanying a Christmas story published in December 1872.

been agitating for ten years when Europe, but not England, was torn by revolution in 1848. The view that labour was the cause of all wealth – 'consequently the working classes have created all wealth' – had been heard before the end of the 1820s; and throughout the whole sequence of industrial development there were 'combinations' and 'strikes' which require to be related both to structural conflicts of economic interest and to the rhythms of boom and slump, 'good' and 'bad' years. 'The kindlier feelings are extinguished [during 'strikes'],' wrote one economic pamphleteer, 'secret leagues are formed, property is destroyed, such of the operatives as do not join the combination are daily assaulted and at length licence mocks the law with the excesses of popular tumult.' His conclusion, like that of the political economist, Nassau Senior, was that 'the more deserving and intelligent portions of the labouring class are often controlled by the greater boldness and activity of that portion which has least knowledge and virtue.'

This pamphleteer recognized that 'the operative population' constituted 'one of the most important elements of society, and when numerically considered, the magnitude of its interests and the extent of its power assume such vast proportions that the folly which neglects them is allied to madness.' He was pleading in fact for social integration, albeit on the assumption made by Senior that 'if the ruling power of any community allows other authorities to frame rules affecting, in their daily habits, their employment and their properties, large bodies of men . . . to affix to the breach of these rules penalties . . . and to proceed to inflict . . . punishments, that ruling power has abdicated its functions so far as respects those among its subjects whom it has surrendered to its self-constituted rivals.'

Yet neither Senior nor the pamphleteer took account of the fact that working men had no share in that 'ruling power' – that was what the Chartists were asking for. Nor could they shape policies designed either to protect or to advance their interests. From what the pamphleteer would have regarded as 'the opposite side', William Pare, the Birmingham co-operator, in an 1850 Preface to a new edition of William Thompson's *Inquiry into the Principles of the Distribution of Wealth most Conducive to Happiness*, first published in 1824, complained that the existing social 'system' could not be called 'society', 'for instead of its being a union of many for one general interest, it is a grotesque assemblage seeking to take advantage of each other's ignorance and helplessness. It is not a wise and scientific association, but a rude, unskilful agglomeration.'

The subsequent story of integration at the local and national level is a complex and in places still controversial one, and it had not gone far by 1851, when the Great Exhibition made the most of what integration already existed. One thing was certain by then, however, as Prince Albert, who played an active part in the preparations for the Exhibition, always insisted. Labour and enterprise had both contributed to Britain's economic success. As noted above, a traveller of the 1850s could claim proudly that 'one million of our working men do more work in a twelvemonth – act more, think more, produce more, live more as active beings in the world, than any three millions in Europe in the same space of time.' The traveller had not visited the United States. In America the story was already a different one, although the workers there also were at the centre of it.

99

98 A conference of engineers at the Menai Straits, in the shadow of the then unfinished Britannia tubular bridge (cf. *ill. 110*). In this group Robert Stephenson, the bridge's designer, is shown seated (centre), and (far right) Isambard Kingdom Brunel, who advised on the methods to be used for floating the giant tubes into position; mezzotint by James Scott after John Lucas, 1858.

99 *Opposite*. The preparations for the Great Exhibition of 1851 were supervised by a group of Commissioners under the chairmanship of Prince Albert, shown (in this painting by H.W. Phillips) seated facing the viewer. The five figures surrounding the Prince are (from right to left): Robert Stephenson; Lord Derby (seated); Sir Robert Peel; Lord John Russell; and Joseph Paxton – the architect of the Crystal Palace.

100 The group portrait, *Men of Progress*, painted *c.* 1860 by Christian Schussele, includes many well-known American figures, some of whose names have become household words. Among the nineteen inventors are (numbered from the left): Samuel Colt, inventor of the revolver (3); Cyrus McCormick, whose reaper revolutionized farming practice (4); Charles Goodyear, who discovered the process of vulcanizing rubber (6); and Samuel Morse, whose telegraph system revolutionized long-distance communications (13).

Mines and miners

101–103 In the early days of coal-mining women were employed in sorting and sifting on the surface (above), but the underground tasks were always allocated to men and ponies; the coal, brought in baskets to the foot of the shaft, was then winched to the surface (below). Colliery wagonways (right) were one of the earliest examples of railed transport.

104–106 The narrowness of the shaft created the need for a special harness to lower a pony into the pit, and in continental mines prayers were said before the miners went down to undertake their dangerous work.

The success achieved by the miners in 'winning the coal' was celebrated on special occasions, such as this open-air fête in 1851 (below) beside the pit-head on the Rhondda branch of the Taff Vale Railway.

Working environments

107–109 The concept of factory work could mean a small number of people supervising large machines (as in the textiles industry, top) or many people performing identical tasks (finishing precision-made metal objects such as hooks and needles) with belt-driven powered machinery. The development of effective underground sewerage systems created a new type of work that no machine could perform – flushing the sewers (as illustrated in Henry Mayhew's *London Labour and London Poor*, 1864).

Opposite
110, 111 Machines could not eliminate the element of heavy physical labour in activities such as iron-founding and mining, as illustrated by a view of the Lymington Ironworks in Northumberland in 1835, and the interior of the Dolcoath tin-mine in Cornwall in 1893.

Construction workers and methods

112–115 The documentation of railway construction is considerable, from the informality of J.C. Bourne's sketches of work on the London and Birmingham Railway in the 1830s (left) to illustrations in official reports on such matters as safety at work (right), with particular reference to the 'navvies' and techniques of excavation.

Bridge-building, as for example in the case of the Britannia tubular bridge over the Menai Straits (below), demanded not only engineering skills of the highest order, but great organizing ability; the tubes, seen here during construction in 1849 near the site, had first to be floated out on pontoons before being raised into position. In London, the building of the underground railways – in this case the Metropolitan Railway – required deep excavations and much temporary shoring as work proceeded.

116 An evocation of life on the footplate – a nineteenth-century engraving entitled 'Seventy miles an hour' – reveals the sense of purpose and urgency expected of both driver and fireman at the controls of an express train.

Opposite
117 Pride in both the uniform and the job was a characteristic of railway staff, as this title-page illustration from a song-sheet makes clear.

118 Joseph Wright of Derby has been described as
'the first professional painter to express the spirit of the
Industrial Revolution'. Among his best-known works
depicting scenes of industry in the broadest sense is
The Iron Forge, painted in 1772.

IT WAS in the United States that a shortage of men led – at an early stage in the story – to an increasing investment in machines, standardized machines with interchangeable parts and a high rate of obsolescence. As Michel Chevalier put it in 1839, 'In Europe work is often wanting for the hands: here in the United States hands are wanting for the work.' An English Parliamentary report of 1854 noted that American workmen hailed 'with satisfaction all mechanical improvements, the importance and value of which, as releasing them from the drudgery of unskilled labour, they are enabled by education to understand and to appreciate.' English workmen by contrast were said to have 'less sympathy with the progress of invention'.

In England, many machines had a monumental quality, and when profits were not being made out of them they were treated with awe, admired or feared rather than welcomed. The great water-wheel (1820) at Styal was said to have 'a slow and stately revolution'. (Samuel Grey's Quarry Bank Mill, now in the possession of the National Trust, has a Director interested in making Styal into a museum which will reveal the story of the part played by cotton in the industrial revolution.) And decades later, a Victorian biographer of Sir Titus Salt, founder of Saltaire (see above, p. 66), stressed that Salt's imposing new mill was 'exactly half the length of St. Paul's [Cathedral in London]'. 'At last', he said of its opening in 1853, 'the great steam engines began to move, sending their motive power into every part of the vast system which, as if touched by a mysterious hand, wakes up into life, the complicated wheels begin to revolve, the ponderous frames to quiver, the spindles to whirl and the shuttles to glide. Now the silence of the place is broken by the din of machinery. . . . How animated the scene!'

Eloquent though the description is, at least down to the last trite comment, it tells us nothing about the details of the technical processes. We are lost in mystery – even in awe. There had been an element of this kind in accounts of industrial processes from the beginning, and emphasis on the 'secrets' and the magic. John Evelyn had included in his list of processes which the Royal Society intended to investigate in the seventeenth century 'Curious Exotick and very rare seacretts', and Darby certainly kept his secrets at Coalbrookdale. Erasmus Darwin once told Matthew Boulton in 1767, 'I have been into the Bowels of old Mother Earth, and seen Wonders and learnt much curious Knowledge in the Regions of darkness.' Darwin not only thought of nymphs and salamanders moving machinery: there were even more elemental forces at work.

> Quick moves the balanced beam, of giant-birth,
> Wields his large limbs, and nodding shakes the earth.

Inventors were 'conjurors' not only for Darwin but for Boulton and many of his customers. There was even a touch of mystery in the whole notion of the Engineer making Engines 'for raising of Water by Fire', although John

4 Processes

Campbell, who used this phrase in defining 'engineer' in his *London Tradesman* (1747), brought the subject back to earth when he wrote that the successful engineer must have 'a solid, not a flighty Head, otherwise his business will tempt him to many useless and expensive projects.'

Stripping away the mystery and the awe, it could be stated in 1818 that whereas it might be thought that 'much skill in mechanics would be necessary to enable a country gentleman to judge of the merits of new machinery and to explain their principles to illiterate uninformed neighbours and tenants . . . in fact the knowledge necessary for this purpose is so easy and comprised in so small a compass that a few hours well employed are sufficient for the purpose.' By then, too, illiterate and hitherto uninformed workers were dealing with machines as a matter of routine.

It is wiser, perhaps, in contemplating processes, to start with the people rather than with the machines – and this despite the fact that Andrew Ure in his *Philosophy of Manufactures* and Edward Baines in his *History of the Cotton Manufacture* (both published in 1835) thought of the people as merely 'attending' on 'series of mechanism', supplying it with work, oiling its joints and checking its 'slight and infrequent irregularities'.

Country gentlemen, often living in remote places far away from 'the populous industrial districts', might by 1818 be using pumps, improved ploughs (a steel ploughshare was put on the market in 1803), seed-drills (James Cooke had produced a new drill in 1782), hoes of various kinds, reaping-machines (the first patent was taken out in 1800), threshing-machines and mechanized barn equipment. Yet even in the middle of the nineteenth century there were districts like the Sussex Weald, where the most antiquated implements were still being used. In 1861 the Isle of Wight was said to be 'a century behind in practical agriculture'. Scythes were still being used in Nottinghamshire and Leicestershire, and sickles in Hertfordshire. Machines had no place at all in fruit- and hop-growing in Kent and Worcestershire, although mechanized industries were now dependent on their products.

Agriculture in 1851 was still employing directly more than a quarter of men of twenty years of age or more, and there were large numbers of carpenters, smiths and ploughwrights. Whereas in 1750 most farm tools (varying significantly in form and name from one part of the country to another) were made locally by the carpenters, smiths, ploughwrights and the farmers themselves, by 1800 farm equipment was being manufactured increasingly in factories, some of these the successors of eighteenth-century craft establishments.

The very notion of agriculture as an industry was certainly an expression of the sense of economic and social transformation, and there were visible symbols of it in the mid-Victorian years in steam-ploughs and 'cable cultivation'. John Fowler (1826–64) was one of the leading pioneers. In 1960, Clark C. Spence, writing in the United States, where the advance of mechanized agriculture was faster, more complete and ultimately decisive, called his book on nineteenth-century agriculture in Britain *God Speed the Plough: The Coming of Steam Cultivation in England.*

There were other applications of power, too, some of them looking to the past, some to the future. In 1851, with the help of steam-pumps, William Wells drained the 1,900-acre Whittlesey Mere in Norfolk so quickly that it was said that a fenman was left stranded in his boat and that fish were dying in the ooze. Meanwhile, railways influenced agriculture almost as much as 'industry' – lowering costs, speeding up deliveries and obviating cattle-driving to the urban markets. Developments in urban drainage helped developments in field drainage: a new tile drainpipe went into industrial production in 1843.

You could read all about 'improved farming', one of Sir Robert Peel's favourite causes, in the *Farmer and Stockbreeder* which began publication in the same year (though the periodical *The Farmer's Magazine* had been launched as early as 1776). The attitudes of farmers – and landowners – were changing throughout the whole period, although there was no consistency of response. Professor D. C. Moore, among others, has pointed to a fundamental dichotomy within the rural ranks at the time of the repeal of the Corn Laws in 1846 – often conceived of, not least at the time, as the triumph of the new industrial over the traditional agricultural interests. On the one hand, there were 'high farmers', who were so increasing their yields and reducing their costs that they could make profits which drove their neighbours to despair. On the other hand, there were farmers who for a whole number of reasons (including bad land; inadequate capital; legal impediments; narrowness of horizons) could neither expand output nor cut costs. Richard Cobden was not unaware of this dichotomy which became more serious as the century went by.

Some of the most important 'industrial processes' throughout the period were directly related to agriculture – and many indirectly. Milling was still an industry divided between water and steam – with a number of large mills in 1851 each employing more than fifty people. (Only two employed more than a hundred.) Brewing had been 'capitalized' in the eighteenth century, and already by 1760 Truman, Hanbury and Buxton's Brewery in Spitalfields (London) was one of the largest factory plants in the country. Steam-engines were soon introduced into it, and although it depended directly on agricultural products, like malt and hops, it lent itself to new modes of production. By 1851 there were some very large units: five of them employed more than a hundred people. The water they depended on was as important in determining the quality of their product, and this in itself accounts for the rise of Burton-on-Trent as a brewing centre, particularly after the railway arrived there in 1839.

Water collection, treatment and distribution constituted one of the key issues of the whole period, particularly from the 1830s onwards when there was an increasing interest in public health (and pollution), and the building – over decades – of vast underground networks of pipes and drains (there were bitter arguments about their design) was one of the greatest of Victorian engineering achievements. As early as 1793 a toast at a dinner of the Smeatonian Society of Civil Engineers was 'success to waterworks, public or private, that contribute to the comfort or the happiness of mankind'.

Food-production processes were industrialized less effectively, but there was one precocious development, rightly singled out by Giedion and others. Samuel Bentham, youngest brother of Jeremy Bentham, was Inspector-General of the Navy Works from 1795 to 1807, and in his care at Deptford was a factory for the production of ship's biscuits. The dough was worked by machine and distributed on what now would be called assembly-line principles to a moulder, a marker, a splitter, a checker and a depositor who each worked with 'the regularity of a clock'.

Such processes pointed to the future. So, too, did the one new industrial process associated with agriculture. John Bennett Lowes began to manufacture mineral superphosphates in 1842, and twelve years later a Frenchman could claim – with great exaggeration – that English farmers were 'already familiar with all the technical terms. They talk of ammonia and phosphates like professed chemists.'

Interest in chemistry (which was eventually to introduce into the world entirely new materials and products divorced from the world of agriculture or nature) was held then to be the link between the arts and the sciences, and however much farmers might know or not know about it, there was great interest in it in cities like Manchester and Birmingham from the time of the Lunar Society onwards. The role of 'pure science' in the industrial revolution continues to be disputed. 'There was practically no exchange of ideas between the scientists and the designers of industrial processes', Lord Ashby has argued, but there has recently been dissent based on detailed studies both of Manchester and Birmingham. What is certain is that bad science as well as good science might guide practical action. Thus, Nicolas Leblanc's soda-making process was based on erroneous analogies with iron-smelting, while C.L. Berthollet's process for using chlorine for bleaching, a key process in the expansion of the textiles industry, was well founded. What is certain, too, is that James Keir's alkali works at Birmingham (for soap-making) was an important innovation. Keir was a friend of Boulton, and wrote his memoir. Equally important, he was a friend also of Joseph Priestley, whose contribution to 'pure science' is beyond doubt.

Keir opened a colliery also, and coal-mining, an extractive industry, for centuries only little influenced by science, was a key industry of the industrial revolution. 'To understand coal is to understand industrialization,' Professor J. U. Nef, a specialist in the early history of the industry, has written; 'to study the history of this great industry is to become increasingly aware of its relation to other industries and, indeed, to the whole historical fabric of industrial civilization.'

The oldest mines had used very simple techniques, and some old 'pits' were either visible outcrops or very shallow, just below the surface of a field. 'Drift mines', like those in recent use in the Forest of Dean where small-scale mining is still practised, recall ancient mining operations. During the eighteenth and nineteenth centuries production was greatly increased. Output rose, indeed, from 6·2 million tons in 1770 to 11 million in 1800, 22·4 million in 1830 and 49·4 million in 1850. As coal production increased, new, deeper seams were tapped.

125–129   Boring was the first process associated with coal-mining, and it changed little for a century or more until in 1804 James Ryan introduced a method of allowing cores to be withdrawn for examination. Shaft-sinking was the second process, and here, as in boring, the most important changes came with the introduction of power-driven devices. (As late as 1898, however, one pit, Prince Pit, Pemberton Colliery, was still using sinkers' tools of the early nineteenth century.) The third process was winning the coal at the coal-face, but there were few changes here in either of the two traditional methods used – the 'bord-and-pillar' method, employed in Durham and Northumberland, whereby one man worked alone undercutting coal with a pick, a crowbar or a wedge, and the 'longwall' method employed in the Midlands, whereby a team of men worked at the coal-face – except that 'longwall' came to replace 'bord-and-pillar' in mining districts where both systems had earlier been employed, and that the use of explosives was introduced. The fourth process was carrying coal from the face to the shaft. In the Scotland of the 1840s, at the end of the period covered in this volume, it was still common for women to carry the coal in baskets, but in other colliery districts, even at the beginning of the period, sledges had long been in use. The coal was carried in 'corves'. Rails of various kinds (and inclined planes) followed (wheeled trams were being used in the Sheffield district by 1790), and so did various improved forms of motive power – women, children, asses, ponies and horses giving way only gradually to cranes, engines, trams and locomotives. (As late as 1924 over 65,000 pit ponies and horses were at work underground.)

The fifth process was winding, where there had been improvements in horse-powered winding before the first steam-winder, using a Watt engine, was erected in 1784 at Walker Colliery on Tyneside. The older Newcomen engines were often preferred to Watt engines, and were widely used in draining also. In general, progress in winding was slow and the general introduction of 'cages' did not take place until the 1840s. An early nineteenth-century steam-winder was vividly described by a miner: 'The beam of wood; fly and drum, with horns, form the chief ornament; no steam indicator or brake are to be seen; but there is a poking handle, like an iron walking-stick, which on every move makes a rattle and clink-clank enough to frighten a statue. Yet as often as it brought its load to the surface, the banksman would have to run and give the fly-wheel a "lift" with his shoulder.'

10

There was little that was 'scientific' about this set of sounds and images. Yet one new device – the miners' safety-lamp of 1815 – was introduced as a result of the work of a distinguished scientist, Sir Humphry Davy (1778–1829), who had become a Fellow of the Royal Society in 1803. What made this invention interesting was that George Stephenson, then an unknown young engineer, introduced a similar, but not identical invention at the same time. Davy reacted arrogantly to Stephenson's claims: as L. T. C. Rolt has put it, 'it appeared to him inconceivable that an obscure, uneducated working man could possibly have forestalled him'. Both kinds of lamps were, in fact, used thereafter, and both were important in making possible increased output and in reducing the dangers of accidents underground. Mining was a dangerous occupation, and good lighting and improved ventilation were as necessary as improvements at the coal-face or in the transport system. There was one terrifying occasion at the Oaks Colliery near Barnsley in Yorkshire when a sudden influx of gas caused all the Davy lamps to become red-hot and all the Stephenson lamps to go out.

In general, it may be said that the huge increase in coal output necessary to sustain the increased production of power and of industrial products and to permit the speedy development of a railway system did not depend on machinery so much as on an increased labour force – the number of colliers increased by three times between the 1790s and the 1840s – and on the exploitation of bigger and deeper mines. Unlike textile-workers, miners were 'a distinct race, in some measure at war with other ranks of society with whom they have little intercourse'. So, too, were some of the other groups of workers concerned with extracting natural materials. They had to go to the materials wherever they were to be found, not to concentrate themselves in cities where materials could be made available. Their secrets were the secrets not of chemistry, but of geology.

Coal-mining, after all, was one of a cluster of extractive industries, still clearly associated with agriculture. Another was quarrying – either for stone or for slate. Brickmaking was a related process, and H.A. Shannon's 'trade index' 1785–1845, derived from Excise statistics related to brick production, reveals peaks in 1824 and 1847. (The Brick Excise was abolished in 1850.) The use of mechanical processes in brick production, as in coal-mining, came slowly and machinery was only introduced in the mid-nineteenth century. By then, however, the railways had opened up a huge new market for bricks as they had for coal – some of the most famous bricks were George Stephenson's purple engineer's bricks called 'Staffordshire blues' – and there had been interesting developments in the production and use of cement. So-called 'Roman cement' was patented in 1796 and was used by Brunel in the mortar for the Thames Tunnel. Industrial towns and cities could be divided into those dependent mainly on brick and those dependent mainly on stone, the latter 'belonging' more to their surrounding country and in some cases, like Hebden Bridge in Yorkshire, acquiring a special beauty as a result. At the other end of the scale was Dickens's 'Coketown', built out of strident brick.

Timber production and imports were less relevant to Britain's power needs than they ever had been in the country's history once coal and coke had begun to be exploited, and from the eighteenth century onwards iron and other materials (including pottery) were taking the place of wood in the making of a wide range of products, which included rails and lathes. Yet there was an increasing demand throughout the period for both home-produced and imported timber, and Peel drastically slashed the duties on imports in 1845. It is no longer argued by economic historians, as it used to be, that a timber shortage as such provoked eighteenth-century industrialization – Hammersley has suggested that 7,000 acres of woodland could supply a seventeenth-century blast-furnace in perpetuity and 6,000 acres a forge – yet growth would not have been possible unless the demand for iron had been met through the development of new techniques and large additional quantities of coal had been produced. The country was not well endowed with woodland, and there were many areas which recalled Anthony Welldon's comment in 1618 that if Judas had betrayed Christ in Scotland he would have had difficulty in finding a tree on which to hang.

One way of describing the industrial changes which Britain pioneered is to say, as Lewis Mumford did, that they marked a profound shift from the technology of wood, wind and water to the technology of 'carboniferous capitalism'. Another more topical way of looking at the changes is to consider them in terms of energy requirements. By 1850, 3 million horses would have been needed to provide energy equal to that made available by steam-power.

Either angle of approach leads inevitably to a consideration first of the iron industry and second of textiles. Most knowledgeable people, if asked in 1850 – or even in 1780 – to identify the major new technical processes associated with the growth of industry, would have pointed first to iron production and all that went with it and second to that of textiles, mainly cotton.

Iron, the world's most ubiquitous metal, had been worked for centuries, and Samuel Smiles in his *Industrial Biography* (1863) began with two pertinent quotations about it. 'Iron', Francis Horner had written, 'is not only the soul of every other manufacture, but the mainspring, perhaps of civilized society.' 'Were the use of iron lost to us,' John Locke had observed decades before iron production leapt ahead, 'we should in a few ages be unavoidably reduced to the wants and ignorance of the ancient savage Americans; so that he who first made known the use of that contemptible mineral may be truly styled the father of Arts and the author of Plenty.'

In the fifteenth century Leonardo da Vinci had designed iron bridges and Dud Dudley in the seventeenth in *Metallum Mortis* (1665) had claimed to have produced good iron with coal. Yet it was not until Abraham Darby I genuinely achieved at Coalbrookdale what Professor D.S. Landes has called 'a semi-adventitious mix' of fairly clean ore and coke in 1709 that coke-smelted iron became a commercial reality. A letter written in 1775 by Darby's daughter-in-law Abiah records how he switched from charcoal not to 'raw coal', but to 'coal cook'd into cynder, as is done for drying Malt'. He also used sand in his furnace, and in Abiah's memorable words 'if we may compare little things with great – as the invention of printing was to writing, so was the moulding and casting in sand to that of the loom'.

Hitherto, Coalbrookdale had been a 'very barren place, little money stirring among its inhabitants'. Soon it was a hive of industry. The process did not spread widely, however, at first (although by 1788 the number of charcoal furnaces in England and Wales had fallen to 24 and the number of coke furnaces to 53, of which 21 were in Shropshire), and further innovations were necessary before coke-smelted iron could be converted profitably into competitive *wrought* iron. Before 1709, coke had already been used in malting and dyeing, but the problem in the case of production iron had been how to get rid of mineral impurities. Not all coke was as suitable as that employed by the Darbys at Coalbrookdale, and in any case Abraham Darby I was mainly interested in cast iron. Wrought iron is the commercially pure form of iron which can be forged and shaped while hot. Cast iron, also known as pig-iron or blast-furnace metal, is an easily meltable crystalline alloy of iron and other elements, chiefly carbon, phosphorus, silicon and manganese, which can be cast molten into moulds. It is less tensile than wrought iron but more easily compressible. The techniques for making both, as Landes has said, involved a 'kind of cookery'.

Efficient furnaces require powerful draughts; the larger the furnace – and coke lent itself to larger and larger furnaces – the more powerful the draught. Abraham Darby had to modify the bellows at his furnace, therefore. Yet it needed the application of steam-power radically to change the possibilities – a combination of cast-iron blowing cylinders (as used at the Carron Iron Works in Scotland) and rotative steam-engines (which enabled barrows carrying iron to be hauled up inclines). A further major improvement associated with J.B. Neilson was the 'hot blast' – preheating of the air, with great attendant savings in fuel costs and the opportunity of removing any sulphur in the slag. Industrial archaeologists are interested in the survivals of different layers of this technology, as W.K.V. Gale explains in his *Iron and Steel* (1969), a volume in the Longmans Industrial Archaeology Series.

Henry Cort's patents of the 1780s, following experiments in a little forge at Fontley, in Hampshire, far both from Shropshire and the other main

120

iron-producing areas, made possible the cheaper production of good wrought iron. His furnace was 'reverberatory'. Raw coal and low-carbon iron were kept separate in it so that there were few impurities in the product. (Three Coalbrookdale men had thought of much the same idea nearly twenty years earlier.) Because the separate molten iron was stirred with an iron bar, the process – a physically hard one – was known as 'puddling'; and forty years later 'wet puddling' was introduced after experiments by a Black Countryman, Joseph Hall. 'Spongy' iron, decarbonized, could be hammered or shingled at lower cost and was of higher quality. Cort also took out a 'rolling' patent (again the idea was not a new one) involving the use of grooved rolls. In 1839 James Nasmyth conceived of the steam-hammer to reduce physical pressure, but this was adopted only slowly.

Cort's inventions were widely used and made possible the great expansion of the iron industry which was essential if machines were to be manufactured in large quantities, if armaments were to be produced (and for much of the period between 1793 and 1815 Britain was at war), if exports were to rise (and they rose twentyfold between 1815 and 1851) and if iron was to be used increasingly for all kinds of hardware (as it was after 1815). By 1800, 'integrated' ironworks – very different from those at the beginning of the century – might have one or more blast-furnaces, refineries, puddling furnaces, power-hammers and driving-mills. And they were not wholly dependent on water-power. The application of steam-power involved less irregularity in production. But it in turn depended on more ample and regular supplies of coal.

However interesting the history of iron, coal and power, the history of cotton has always been given priority by some historians, including one of the latest, Professor D. S. Landes. 'Looking back from the vantage point of one hundred years or more' of 'living in a world in which heavy industry is the basis of the economy,' he argues, 'writers have tended to over-emphasize the immediate significance for the eighteenth century of the technological advantages in smelting and refining.' It was cotton which really marked the transformation – new material and new product; new interlocking processes, based on division of labour; new scale of plant; critical exports.

Certainly from the vantage point of the 1850s there was little doubt about this. 'The successive introduction of the water-frame, the spinning jenny, the mule and the power loom', exclaimed Henry Dunckley, prize-winner of 1854 for an essay on free trade, *The Charter of the Nations*, 'produced a total change in the textile manufactures. A still higher place must be assigned to the steam engine, an invention which seems the necessary complement of every other.' And here the rhetoric burst out, for in addition the steam-engine 'renders every art prolific and arms the softest touch of genius with demiurgic power.' The joint effect of different textiles inventions on the progress of trade more resembled 'the marvels of romance . . . than the sober facts of industry'. Cotton was a 'wondrous plant' which had become 'one of the principal agents of civilization'. 'Its useful lustre was wisely reserved till the close of the feudal epoch, as if to show that the decaying institutions of the middle ages would not involve in their ruin the extinction of society; that their overthrow would rather resemble the release of an imprisoned soul.'

To move back from language of this kind to technical descriptions of interrelated textiles processes is to descend quickly to the earth. And it should be stated at once that flowery talk of 'the release of an imprisoned soul' was contemporaneous with crude talk of the factory operatives as 'hands'. Production of woollen textiles, as Dyer had recognized, had already involved a long chain of processes before the industrial revolution – wool sorting and cleaning; wool-combing (men's work – and hard work at that); spinning, weaving, fulling (an operation transferred to mills early in industrial history (see p. 64), tentering (or stretching), bleaching, dressing (usually carried out in jig-mills); and dyeing. Before the water-frame, the first invention on Dunckley's list, Thomas Lombe had devised machines to throw silk, John Kay, the Lancashire clockmaker (see above, p. 110) had invented the flying shuttle (1733), which enabled a single weaver to make cloth of a width that had previously required two men (the flying shuttle, mounted on wheels, was struck by hammers and driven through the warp); and Lewis Paul had introduced improvements into 'spinning' (passing carded fibres through two sets of rollers revolving at different speeds).

It is customary to treat 'the wave of inventions' in the eighteenth-century cotton revolution (which for various reasons pre-dated those in the older woollen industry) as being directly interrelated. Just as inventions in the furnace (smelting) were followed by inventions in the forge (refining), so inventions in weaving, beginning with Kay's flying shuttle, the first new device for centuries in the history of the loom, put pressure on spinners to produce more yarn. At the beginning of the eighteenth century – so the argument runs – weaving was more 'productive' than spinning – it took three spinners to supply each weaver – and Kay (though he had to flee to France as a result of his achievement) tilted the balance still further. (In fact, the flying shuttle did not come into general use until after 1760.) Hargreaves's spinning-jenny (1764–7) was one 'response' only to the spinning challenge (a neighbour, Thomas Highs, claimed to have preceded him), particularly useful in that it could be used inside the home and within the framework of a domestic rather than a factory economy. Yet the jenny ('jenny', like 'ginny' or 'gin', was a contraction of the word 'engine') did not meet the whole of the problem because of the softness of jenny-spun yarn which could not be used for the weaver's warp. Arkwright's water-frame (1768; patented 1779, a fiercely contested patent which was cancelled in 1785) and Samuel Crompton's 'mule' (1772–3), a combination of jenny and water-frame, offered a more promising future; and the challenge now passed back from the spinners to the weavers. Cartwright's power loom (1786) was the answer, although there were power-driven looms before that – one 1774 patent was for a loom 'which may be worked by men, horses, cattle, fire or water' – and it was not until further improvements had been made by William Radcliffe, who owned a mill at Mellor in Cheshire, that looms began to be worked economically and 'the factory system', 'a new system of manufacture', established itself. Both spinning and weaving thereafter began to be concentrated in factories or 'sheds', each with its own engine-house. Some were severely *136* 'functional' in character, as were the great warehouses: they have been *178* sympathetically described by J. M. Richards in his *Functional Tradition as shown in Early Industrial Buildings* (1958). Others reflected the tastes, even the fantasies, of the manufacturer. The context of work must always be considered as well as the processes of manufacture.

It is wise not to romanticize 'hand production' as opposed to machine production. 'The hand-spun yarn manufacture', stated a former Leeds worsted-manufacturer in his eighties, writing towards the end of the eighteenth century, 'was an anxious and laborious occupation, requiring the eyes and hands of the master in several processes.' 'Independence' was never absolute. Children's work, moreover, was often faulty work: 'in sorting out yarns we not only met with whole hanks clumsily spun, but, not seldom, good and bad reeled in the same hank.' Factory employment is difficult to generalize about. There were thought at the time to be 'good' and 'bad' employers, and in recent years considerable attention has been paid by historians to methods of oversight and management. Factory rules were often set out precisely, and fines were imposed on those workers who broke them. 'Taming' a new labour force was felt to be at least as difficult as 'taming' nature.

One group of workers depended on another. Thus, spinners could operate efficiently only if other methods of carding were introduced. Arkwright had brought into operation carding by cylinders, a process which required power – first water-power, and later (after a delay) steam. T.S. Ashton has considered this rolling process in terms of a transfer from the iron to the textiles industry; others have suggested, however, that roller drawing-out developed from watching a spinster at the wheel. In any case the Society of Arts in 1761 offered prizes for the invention of a machine which would 'spin six threads of wool, flax, hemp or cotton [materials which required different treatment] at one time and that will require but one person to work and attend it.'

So many processes were involved in the textiles industry that the internal interactions were themselves complex. Decades before Arkwright, Lewis Paul (and John Wyatt) had devised spinning-machines (Birmingham, not Manchester, was Paul's centre), and Dyer described in *The Fleece* (1757):

> A circular machine of new design
> In conic shape; it draws and spins a thread
> Without the tedious task of needless hands.

Erasmus Darwin was equally lyrical about Arkwright's roller spinner, which obviously impressed contemporaries.

The most recent historian of textiles technology, W. English, however, has devoted more attention than contemporaries did to other textiles processes and machines – those for opening and cleaning cotton, for example, the first of them 'scutching and blowing machines'. The initial stages in preparing cotton took place, of course, far away from Britain – to an increasing extent in the American South, and it was in 1794 that Eli Whitney patented his cotton-gin for removing seeds from the raw cotton. With one man and a horse, it could do the work previously done by fifty men.

The idea of horse-power was carried over from the field to the factory. George Ewart Evans's *The Horse in the Furrow* (1960) tells what happened to the horse in the fields. Meanwhile, however, factories were not laboratories, nor did they have laboratories attached to them. Steam-engines were made *before* scientists understood much about the laws of thermodynamics because practical men appreciated at once the increase in power they offered, as well as the increase in reliability. Nor did steam-power oust water-power. Savery and Newcomen engines were used to

153

pump water to operate water-wheels even though they could not be used to drive a mill directly, and wind- and water-power continued to be used in the nineteenth century. The logic of what was happening took time to be appreciated. Trevithick's high-pressure engines were used before there was any thought of a railway system.

It is impossible adequately to consider questions of processes in textiles or in the iron industry without relating technology to economics – changes in the costs of inputs (including wages) and in the prices of products. 'Machines either save material, or diminish labour or both' (Babbage). In considering the economics, it is necessary to take into account transport and distribution costs as well as profit margins when looking at the relationship between factory (or mine) costs and market prices.

The calculations are sophisticated, but inevitably there were protagonists and critics of the competitive system who did not bother about the sophistication. 'It is better to have a population of men than of steam engines' was one cry, to which the response (without essential qualifications both about 'temporary distress' and continuing economic fluctuations) was 'as the productions of industry multiply, the means of acquiring their productions multiply also'. Nor were general comments of this kind restricted to the relationship between men and machines. Employers interested in acquiring steam-engines in the 1780s had to balance the high capital costs of Watt engines against the high rate of coal consumption of Newcomen engines (except when working in coal-mines, where coal was cheap). And even in coal-mines the advantages of the Watt engine could not be overlooked. Thus, when at the Bloomfield Colliery near Dudley, employers met with 'a number of scientific gentlemen' to see Boulton and Watt's first commercial pumping engine, 'The Parliament Engine', they were deeply impressed by the fact that 'so singular and powerful a machine' used only 'one fourth of the fuel that a common engine would require to produce the same quantity of power.'

Royalty on Boulton and Watt engines was calculated on the basis of one-third of the annual cost of coal saved by not using a Newcomen engine. Yet James Watt jun. observed in the Manchester of 1790 that machines were being constructed locally 'upon the old plan' on grounds of capital cost. Only the larger firms were able to afford Boulton and Watt engines.

The technology itself, of course, had its own momentum. The engines of 1790 depended on machine production of a specialization and refinement which was absent in the days of the early Savery and Newcomen engines. Steam-power, reciprocating (as in the original engines, as used in 1726 in the York Buildings Waterworks near Charing Cross) or rotative (as in the engines being made for the new Albion Flour Mill near Blackfriars Bridge in 1786), could not have been applied to different sectors of industry had it not been for the discovery of new ways of boring iron and of working it in other ways. John Wilkinson's patent for boring cannon (1774) could be adapted to the boring of cylinders. And a whole battery of other devices for grinding, slotting, drilling, planing and cutting followed, one of the earliest being Henry Maudslay's slide rest applied to a lathe in 1794. When Watt had moved from Scotland to Birmingham, Smeaton, who considered all existing engines 'too liable to stoppage . . . passing from almost full power and motion to a total cessation', had told him that 'neither tools nor workmen existed that could manufacture so complex a machine [as Watt's early invention] with sufficient precision.' But, by 1800, when the

Watt/Boulton patent expired, this was no longer true. Indeed, as *Rees's Cyclopaedia* put it in 1819, 'As there are immense numbers of each part of every machine to be made, it becomes, in the same way as with the clockmaker, worth the machine-maker's trouble to construct complicated tools and engines to expedite the manufacture of the parts.'

'Expedition' was certainly necessary as the steam-locomotive developed following Richard Trevithick's experiments. Two main technical questions which had to be answered before the locomotive became a practical proposition related first to the operations of the engine and second to the characteristics of the rail. Trevithick appreciated before Stephenson that the boiler fire would be quickened and steam-raising improved by turning the exhaust steam from the cylinders of the engine into the chimney and, as L. T. C. Rolt puts it, 'if necessary contracting the outlet to sharpen the blast'. It was before the 1829 Rainhill speed trials that Thomas Gray wrote in his *Observations on a General Iron Railway* that 'the man who can *now hesitate* to recommend steam engines instead of horse power must be pitied for his ignorance or despised for his obstinacy'.

The problem of the rail itself took time and much testing to solve. *61* William Hedley of Wylam Colliery claimed that it was he, and not Stephenson, who 'established the principle of locomotion by the friction or adhesion of the wheels upon the rails' in 1813. It was Stephenson, however, whose *Blücher* first proved that locomotives could move along cast-iron rails that were tough enough and hard enough to bear the weight. Until 1821 the sole alternative to cast-iron rails was the use of square-section wrought-iron bars, which could be used only on light narrow-gauge tramways in mines. In 1821, however, John Birkinshaw of Bedlington, near Morpeth, patented wrought-iron rails of 15-ft lengths.

An argument about the respective merits of cast and wrought iron ensued and was just as bitter as the argument about the width of the gauge in the 1840s, when Stephenson, with his narrower gauge of under 5 ft (the width of some tracks in his backyard along which his horse used to draw small trucks, and the one which was eventually adopted as the standard gauge of 4 ft 8½ in), and Brunel – with his stately gauge of 7 ft – were pitted against each other. (Brunel's Great Western Railway did not convert fully to the standard gauge until 1892, over thirty years after his death.)

Stephenson continued to believe after 1814 that additional tractive power was necessary on inclines and, distrusting the adhesive power of the locomotive, included plans for such assistance on three sections of incline on the route of the Liverpool and Manchester Railway. The locomotive and the iron rail both proved themselves in practice, however, and the line was relaid in 1837 with 50-lb rails supported on timber sleepers throughout. The first passengers on the line spoke most of the sensations of travelling at speed. 'The engineer opens the valves, the hissing of steam is suppressed, the engine moves and is heard to pant, not from exhaustion, but impatient of restraint, the blazing cinders fall from behind it and the trail of carriages is dragged along with a sudden and agreeable velocity, becoming, as it were, the tail of a comet.'

The railways not only enlivened personal sensation: they stimulated the whole of the economy, not merely the iron and coal trades. The labour force actually engaged in construction reached 100,000 in 1840 and as many as 300,000 by the time the railway mania burst. Their cost, met entirely by private enterprise, was high – more than three times more per mile than the American and European railways. Yet they drew out new skills and made possible new developments in retailing, the communication of messages and the use of leisure. In 1838 the Directors of the Great Western approved the installation of the electric telegraph (Charles Wheatstone's patent had been granted a year before) between Paddington and West Drayton, a distance of thirteen miles, and this was extended to Slough in 1842. One of the first excursion trains – from London to Brighton – ran two years later at Easter 1844, when three engines hauled thirty-eight coaches and took 4½ hours to make the journey.

Some of the new technical processes associated with industrialization were designed to make 'consumers' happier even in a bleak age and some to make them less ignorant in an age when there was still no system of education provided by the State or by local authorities.

Pottery-making, an industry directly related to the needs and tastes of domestic consumers, had developed in the 'Potteries' district, centred on Stoke-on-Trent, before Wedgwood. Fine salt-glazed stoneware, almost a porcelain, associated with the name of John Astbury (1688?–1743) had enjoyed great popularity between 1710 and 1780. It was Astbury, too, who was said to have introduced a new material, ground flint, into pottery production (and flint was an essential ingredient in Wedgwood's creamware, first developed *c.* 1760).

'Like every industry,' John Thomas has written (1937), 'pottery, even in the peasant stage, needs raw materials. These must be suitably prepared, or the finished article will be poor. All these peasant potters had raw materials prepared in water mills. These were often converted corn mills. These flint water mills have persisted from the seventeenth century to this day in the Potteries.' Steam-power was used in flint and glazing mills, and by the 1770s local clays had been abandoned and improvements had been made in moulding and casting (plaster of Paris moulds were introduced in 1745), in the wheel ('jollies' or 'jiggers' were used to shape mass-produced wares), in the ovens (which became larger and provided more even temperatures) and in methods of decoration (enamelling and transfer-printing, etc.). According to Thomas, Josiah Wedgwood, in particular 'elevated pottery manufacture from a matter of guess-work and procedure by rule of thumb to a matter of scientific method and calculation'. There were many potters pushing further the division of labour, but Wedgwood pushed furthest in the extension of marketing both at home and abroad. He took out only one patent (to produce 'encaustic gold bronze'), but he wanted, in his own words, 'to make such machines of the Men as cannot err'. He did not compete with other potters in reducing prices, however, but rather encouraged quality – and fashion. '*Fashion* is infinitely superior to *Merit* in many respects' was one of his business aphorisms. As Neil McKendrick has written, 'He was what he wished to be: Vase Maker General to the Universe.'

In the glass industry, home production was encouraged by a doubling of excise duty on imported glass, but consumption was limited by the heavy duties levied on windows and other goods. The window tax was halved in 1823, but not abolished until 1851. Meanwhile, the great change was the move after the 1830s from crown glass, the earliest method of making sheet glass by hand, to glass made by blowing and cutting a cylindrical bubble, first devised in France and Germany and brought to England in 1832. The process, which enabled glass to be used for larger panes, required great

Stacking pottery in a kiln in preparation for firing; although the nature of the product still called for careful handling, industrialization greatly increased output and this in turn led to the use of much larger kilns than before.

skill, and five specialized groups of skilled workers were involved – gatherers, blowers, snappers, cutters and flatteners. Meanwhile, cast plate-glass making (originally a French process) was increasingly concentrated in St Helens, where coal was cheap and plentiful. The casting hall there, 113 yards long by 50 yards wide, built in 1776, was one of the biggest industrial buildings in Britain. Yet a hall nearly twice as big with two founding and two firing kilns was built – also at St Helens – by the Union Plate Glass Works in 1836/7. Improvements were made in the 1830s and 1840s, notably in methods of grinding, smoothing and polishing sheet glass 'to remove the irregularities of surface' and to give it a better sheen, and in kiln-construction. Chance Brothers in Smethwick (with strong American connections) was the main centre of innovation, also acquiring key French patents, like one for stirring (1837) which was not fully exploited until the 1840s. The use of coal instead of wood transformed the eighteenth-century industry, and the use of cast-iron casting tables after 1843 was equally revolutionary. There were dramatic changes in colouring techniques also, not always aesthetically pleasing. As early as 1751, indeed, a traveller had described Stourbridge as 'famous for its glass manufacture, which is here coloured in the liquid of all the capital colours in their several shades'.

No survey of industrial processes, however brief, would be complete without reference to paper. Without paper, after all, the whole rhetoric of early industrialization would have disappeared into the air. And there was plenty of rhetoric about paper itself. Richard Cobden was not alone in starting his chronicle of useful inventions with the printing-press, and the Excise duty on paper (first levied in 1712, halved in 1737, not repealed until 1861), was generally described as 'a tax on knowledge'.

The price of paper – much in demand for multiple uses – doubled between 1793 and 1801, giving an incentive to the development of new techniques of production, and the Society for the Encouragement of Arts, Manufactures and Commerce was not alone in offering premiums for patents involving the use of materials other than rags in the basic paper pulp. Bleaching rags with chlorine had already been introduced into paper-making (1792) as well as textiles, but it was not until the 1860s that wood was generally used in paper-making in Britain, almost two decades after Heinrich Vöelter (1846) had patented a new method of using it. There were improvements in paper-making machinery, however. At the beginning of the eighteenth century the pulp was prepared by a stamping method of beating the materials using hammers and mortars, but in the 1790s a French invention, 'the endless web' process, was introduced into Britain at the Frogmore Mills near Hemel Hempstead. The machines were built at Donkin's Bermondsey factory, and some of them were exported, a number of them to the United States. In 1809 John Dickinson, who two years earlier had produced a useful paper-cutting machine, patented a new cylinder machine for paper-making, and in 1815 he introduced a method of steam drying machine-sized paper. He was one of a number of pioneers, but they did not render obsolete the old vat mills which were forced rather to increasing specialization.

Printing changes, sharply reducing costs, diminished the proportionate importance of paper costs in the manufacture of books and newspapers. William Nicholson in 1790 had conceived of a printing-press utilizing rollers for inking – yet another illustration of the importance of rolling techniques in early industrialization – which would supplant the old wooden hand-press. It was not until the end of the century, however, that the Earl of Stanhope's iron presses came into use and not until 1810 that the idea of steam-driven presses (patented by Frederick Koenig) became a reality: appropriately, a sheet of *The Annual Register* was machine-printed in 1811, and three years later John Walter, proprietor of *The Times*, installed two Koenig machines. Other improvements followed on both *139–142* sides of the Atlantic. It was even more appropriate that the Society for the Diffusion of Useful Knowledge, founded in 1827 and from the start nicknamed 'The Steam Intellect Society', printed its books and pamphlets using steam-power. At the end of the 1830s, William Clowes, its printer, had nineteen presses at work, each capable of turning out 1,000 sheets an hour.

The ingenuity of the new processes, the increased output per man, and the speed of the new rhythms of work were extolled by enthusiastic contemporaries, not least when they were questioned or resisted by workers brought up in a new tradition. Yet in retrospect, at least, many of them seemed wasteful of materials and power, first stages only in a process of industrial transformation which, once begun, would go through many phases. Thus, 90 per cent of the heat created by early steam-engines was directly wasted, and there were immense direct wastes of chemicals (for example, hydrochloric acid) in noxious fumes in processes like the Leblanc process. The by-products of coal were wasted for decades, and of every charge of 24 tons of iron ore, limestone and coke making their way into the furnaces of the Black Country, 5 tons went into slag. The social costs were even greater, of course, as the appearance of the Black Country or of most scattered mining villages proved.

Of the 'inventions' themselves, many were practical, on-the-spot improvements and adaptations, what S. C. Gilfillan in his *The Sociology of Invention* (1935) called 'a perpetual accretion of little details, probably having neither beginning, completion nor definable limits'. Only later in most cases – and sometimes much later in the twentieth century – were new 'scientific' procedures introduced which left far behind both 'traditional' techniques and the revised techniques of early industrialization. There was some truth in L. J. Henderson's claim that until 1850 the steam-engine, chief symbol of the new dispensation, 'did more for science than science did for the steam engine'. There were some devices developed or experiments successfully carried out in early industrialization, however, which had distant futures – notably James Watt's 'governor', herald of automation (and itself said to have been borrowed from a Thomas Mead patent for windmills).

Humphry Davy's isolation of sodium and potassium by electrolysis in 1807 pointed to the modern electro-chemical industries, and Sir George Cayley's definition of aerodynamic forces (1799) to modern aviation. (There was a pre-history of the automobile also). Of Cayley (1773–1857) Orville Wright commented in 1912 that 'he knew more of the principles of aeronautics than any of his predecessors, and as much as any that followed him up to the close of the nineteenth century'. Finally it was at the height of the age of steam that the Electrical Society of London, founded in 1837 by William Sturgeon, proclaimed that 'as a universal agent in nature and space electricity takes the first rank in the temple of knowledge'.

Ironworks in Britain and France

119, 121 Before mechanical power took over the strain in heavy industrial processes, much manpower was required in the various stages of producing iron and iron products: in a watercolour by C.W. Campion (above), teams of men are seen at work at the Dowlais rolling-mills, and (opposite) manœuvring a large white-hot ingot from the puddling furnace to the steam-hammer at Le Creusot.

120 In the early stages of iron production, alternate layers of coke and iron ore were tipped into the top of the blast-furnace for smelting. The use of coke in smelting was first developed by Abraham Darby I in 1709; in this engraving, published *c.* 1880, the technique is being used in a fully industrialized situation.

122–124 The spread of the railway system generated a greatly increased demand for iron products, especially rails of uniform length and quality; the shaping of rails was performed (left) by a succession of rollers, as seen in this engraving published *c.* 1880. The production of low-carbon steel was achieved in the 1850s by Henry Bessemer, whose converter (below) worked on the simple principle of blowing air through molten iron to burn out most of the impurities; at first steel ingots were limited in size, but the use of large converters – as at Pittsburgh, Pa (opposite) – led to mass-production of high-quality steel for use in bridges and other construction work.

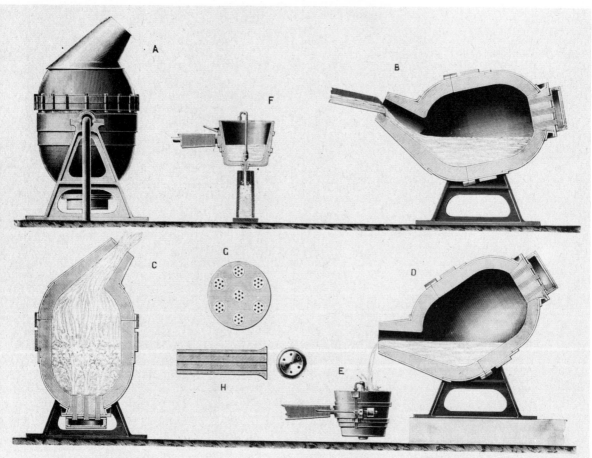

Coal mining

125–127 From the earliest days of deep mining (left) access and ventilation shafts were essential for efficient working; many of the tasks performed by men and horses were later taken over by steam-powered winding engines and steam-hammers for boring (below).

Opposite
128, 129 Two pit-head scenes – an anonymous painting, *c.* 1820, and a sketch by T.H. Hair of the Church Pit, Wallsend, 1839 – show the use of steam-powered pumping engines and winding gear and the progression from horse-drawn wagons to colliery wagonways (in this case the slight incline permits one man to push a loaded wagon with one hand).

Tunnels and mines

130 Railway engineering involved large-scale tunnelling operations, a notable example being the Kilsby Tunnel on the London and Birmingham Railway, for which enormous shafts (left) were sunk for the removal of spoil and to provide ventilation and access for maintenance. This watercolour by J. C. Bourne is one of a series showing the construction work on the line in the 1830s.

131 Open-cast workings such as the Penrhyn slate quarry in Carnarvonshire (below), seen in a lithograph by W. Crane (1842), produced scars in the landscape. Yet they were not without a certain monumental quality of their own.

132, 133 The extraction of
metal ores could be on a fairly
small scale, with the works
blending into the landscape – as
at the Carclase tin-mine in
Cornwall in 1813, with its
water-wheels providing power
for crushing rock – or involve
large-scale operations such as
the Dannemora iron-mine in
Sweden.

153

134–137
The textiles industry was transformed
by the introduction first of water-
powered and then of steam-powered
machinery. At Akroyd's worsted
factory in Yorkshire (left) a series of
Jacquard looms produced patterned
fabrics (as illustrated in the *Penny
Magazine* in 1844), and the use of
rollers (above), facilitated the
continuous printing of patterns on
calico (a dress fabric).

Marshall's flax-mill in Leeds
(opposite) was an important example
of purpose-built industrial architecture
(cf. *ill. 48*), equipped with the latest
spinning-machines. Leather-dressing,
however, was a process that could not
be mechanized, although a well-
planned workshop with gas-lighting
greatly improved working conditions.

Paper and printing

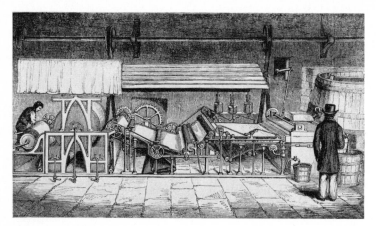

138–142 The ability of machines to produce paper in large quantities (left) and the use of rotary printing-presses revolutionized the production of newspapers and books. The Wharfedale printing-press of 1858 is shown below in a contemporary photograph, and two newspaper presses used for printing *The Times* are contrasted opposite – the Hoe ten-feeder press (right), imported from America in 1857, introduced a considerable degree of automation compared with the earlier type. The operation of Applegarth's steam printing-machine (opposite, below) was demonstrated to the public at the Great Exhibition in 1851.

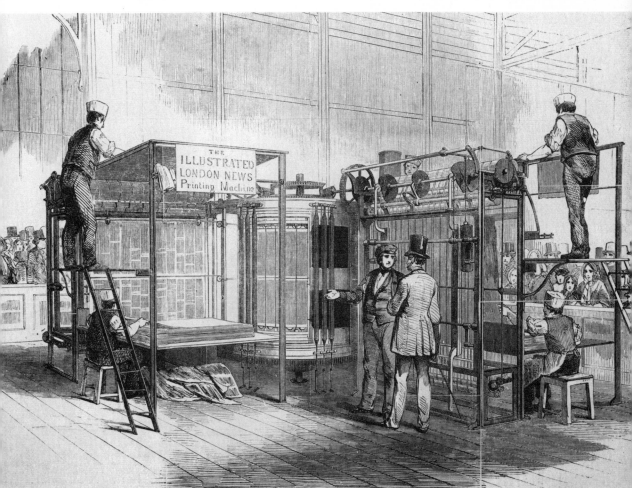

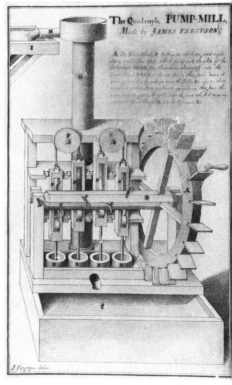

143–145 Before the introduction of steam, water-wheels were a necessary source of power for difficult pumping operations, a notable example being the great wheel (above) used to drive furnace pumps at Benthall, near Coalbrookdale; the principle involved was expounded in lectures by James Ferguson, who in 1773 published a drawing of a hand-operated model employing cams attached to a series of pump rods. A century later, the generation of electricity (right) called for an elaborate system of belt-driven dynamos.

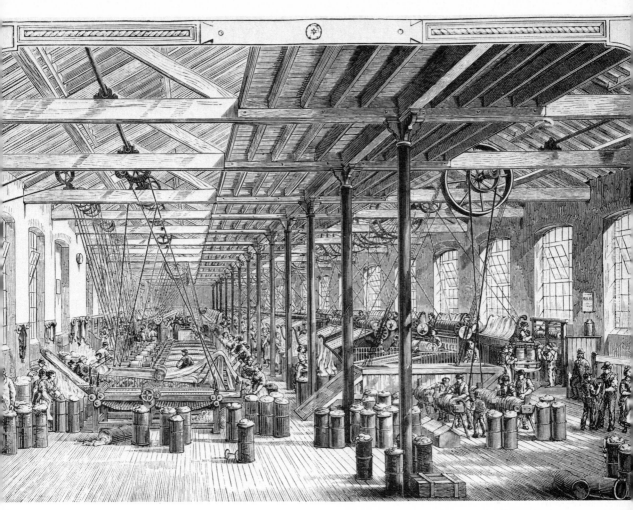

146, 147 By the middle of the century machines had been designed to do all kinds of standardized and repetitive jobs, among them rope-making (above) and moulding bricks – the human element was now more concerned with ensuring the machine's efficiency.

Agriculture

148–150 Among the numerous mechanical aids introduced into farming were the four-wheeled seed-drill invented in 1745 (above) and Crosskill's patent roller (left), shown at the Great Exhibition. The advent of the portable steam-engine not only took much of the strain out of such tasks as threshing (below) but brought the practical use of steam-power to the notice of many country people for the first time.

151, 152 In the United States, the grain harvest was on an altogether different scale, as revealed by the huge elevators in Chicago and the 'whaleback' ship being loaded (below), and by Benjamin Holt's combine-harvester of 1887, drawn by a team of 33 horses.

153 In the Deep South, the cotton crop was picked, cleaned and prepared for shipment by Negro slaves: the pressing of raw cotton into bales is shown (below) in an engraving of *c.* 1855.

Accidents and pollution

154 The extent of disasters cannot be gauged simply from scenes of accidents (below). The missing part of this broken cast-iron beam of a pumping engine at the New Hartley Pit in 1862 blocked the mine-shaft, preventing rescuers from descending, and the failure of the pump also allowed water to flood the mine. In this incident 204 men and boys were drowned.

155 The built-in safety device incorporated by Elisha Otis in his elevator, and demonstrated by him (above), opened the way – in the 1850s and 1860s – for the construction of the first tall buildings using a framework of wrought iron.

156 By 1858, the pollution of the Thames in London had reached such proportions that *Punch* could publish cartoons such as 'The "Silent Highway"-Man'.

Opposite

157, 158 Major industrial hazards included fire, such as that which ravaged a textile-mill at Stockport in 1851, and explosions, particularly in coal-mines where naked lights ignited fire damp (methane gas) – a problem which Humphry Davy helped to overcome with his invention of the safety-lamp.

5 Products

Most of the products of early industrialization were on proud display in the Crystal Palace, which was officially opened by Queen Victoria on May Day 1851. 'It was neither crystal nor a palace', wrote Leigh Hunt, survivor from an older generation. 'It was a bazaar, admirably constructed for its purpose, and justly surprising those who beheld its interior.' The prophet of a newer generation, John Ruskin – and his prophetic status was still not quite established – was less flattering: 'the quantity of bodily industry which that Crystal Palace expresses is very great. So far it is good.' Thackeray caught the general mood rather better in an ode published in *The Times* on opening day. He, for one, made the most of the combination of utilitarian achievement and romance:

> A palace as for fairy Prince,
> A rare pavilion, such as man
> Saw never since mankind began
> And built and glazed.

Thackeray also made the most of the objects 'from Mississippi and from Nile – from Baltic, Ganges, Bosphorus', singling out those from his own country:

> Look yonder where the engines toil:
> These England's arms of conquest are,
> The trophies of her bloodless war:
> Brave weapons these.
> Victorious over wave and soil,
> With these she sails, she weaves, she toils,
> Pierces the everlasting hills
> And spans the seas.

The literature of the Great Exhibition was voluminous, including specialized literature for children and for foreigners and a wide range of *genres* from Martin Tupper's 'Exhibition Hymn' – on sale in thirty languages, with music by Sebastian Wesley – to Charles Babbage's *The Exposition of 1851*, written long before May Day. Thackeray himself wrote not only his *May-Day ode* but *Mr. Molony's Account of the Crystal Palace:*

> There's taypots there,
> And cannons rare;
> There's coffins filled with roses;
> There's canvas tints,
> Teeth insthrumints
> And shuits of clothes by Moses.
>
> There's lashins more
> Of things in store,
> But thim I don't remimber;

Nor could disclose
Did I compose
From May time to Novimber.

The products on display at the Great Exhibition of 1851 had little in common with those which might have been seen on display a century earlier or those which were actually on display at the first exhibition held by the Society for the Encouragement of Arts, Manufactures and Commerce in 1761. In the case of the 1761 Exhibition, however, there was a little of the same sense of pride in ingenuity and willingness to try to meet industrial needs as there was to be in 1851. A threshing-machine was prominent, as was a model of a saw-mill. Several models of windmills and tide-mills could be examined – this is the kind of technology that is returning to fashion in the late twentieth century – and there were spinning-wheels, too, and models of sailing-ships complete with all their rigging. New forms of power were represented only by one 'fire-engine', exhibited briefly by Keane Fitzgerald, F.R.S., the Vice-President of the Society, who later experimented with rotary motion. The machines on display were all worked, as an early member of the staff of the Society put it, not very elegantly,

> . . . by windy Pow'r or wat'ry Force
> Or by circumambulating Horse.

The Society was just as prominent as it had been in 1761 eighty years later when the technology and the social context had both changed. Henry Cole (1808–82), who joined its Council in 1846 – he had won a prize for designing a tea-service a year earlier – had just as strong ideas on design – and far more controversial ones – than Wedgwood (whose successor kept his Classical shapes in 1851). Like Prince Albert, who became President in 1847, Cole believed that there was no going back before the age of machines. He talked enthusiastically of 'wedding' mechanical skill and high art, of 'an alliance between art and manufacture which would promote public taste'. The Society organized a number of exhibitions and encouraged others, and both Cole and the Prince Consort plunged themselves with imagination and vigour into the campaign to hold a great exhibition in 1851.

All patented articles were excluded from this 1761 Exhibition, whereas in 1851 there were many patented products among the 100,000 or more on display. (There were, however, a number of old models also, some going back to the 1790s.) Above all, there was an emphasis on power. At the approach (beyond Charles Crooks's imposing cast-iron gates, made in Coalbrookdale) there was a huge block of coal weighing 24 tons from the Duke of Devonshire's Staveley mines not far from his seat, Chatsworth. James Nasmyth's steam-hammer caught the imagination of visitors more, it was said, than any other object in the Exhibition, although passers-by had been forcibly struck before the Exhibition opened by the sight of the two powerful crab-cranes which hoisted the roof-ribs of the Crystal Palace into position. At the front of the machinery section, which included an area devoted to moving machinery, the great 'hydraulic press' or jack stood out. It was remarkable not only for its size, but because it had made workable various contrivances for holding the chains by which the tubes for the Britannia Bridge, 'a bridge of tubes' over the Menai Straits, were raised. It is fascinating to note the contrast between Robert Stephenson's bridge,

VIII

which included one continuous tube 1,511 ft long, and Telford's Products
suspension bridge, built twenty-four years earlier and situated only a mile
away to the north. Telford's bridge was far more graceful, but
Stephenson's was solid and powerful and its construction had demanded
exceptional engineering skills. Stephenson consulted Fairbairn and
Professor Eaton Hodgkinson about major problems – the latter was the
country's chief authority on iron beams – and Brunel was present when the
first great tube was floated. Stephenson's Resident Engineer, Edwin Clark,
wrote a definitive account of the whole process of construction (recorded
pictorially too) just as Telford's Resident Engineer, William Provis, had
done. The Exhibition commentator of 1851 described the new bridge as
'the triumphal arch of modern engineering'.

This was immediate comment. Yet the commentator went on to relate
size and power to ingenuity and diversity. 'On every side, around this
Stephenson apparatus, thousands of little machines, which well deserved
the epithet of beautiful, were hard at work, and ingeniously occupied in the
manufacture of all sorts of useful articles from knife handles to envelopes.'
'In this Department which might well be called the great park of
machinery,' the author concluded, 'a thoughtful observer could easily
discover the distinctive character of the English nation, as regards political
economy – Englishmen employ their capital, but are ever seeking for
mechanical means to work it.'

The theme had immediate point, for the objects on display at the
Exhibition were symbols of 'visible progress'. The concrete and the
abstract were both stressed, the materialism and the spirit that lay behind
it. The motto of Cole's biography was – very properly – 'whatsoever thy
hand findeth to do, do it with thy might'. The Gospel of Work was extolled:
Exhibition medals bore the words *Pulcher et ille labor palma decorate laborem*.
Universal peace was proclaimed too: *Paxton vobiscum* – a punning reference
to Joseph Paxton (1803–68), the architect of the Palace which was first
sketched by him on a piece of blotting-paper and which was built within a
few months. The Exhibition was purposefully international: it displayed
products from all parts of the world: 7,351 exhibitors came from the British
Isles and Empire, 6,556 from foreign countries. And the fact that Britain
stood out as 'the workshop of the world' did not detract from the
internationalism: it coloured its forms of expression, above all the
internationalism of free trade. A facsimile of an Exhibition minute in the
handwriting of the Prince Consort read: 'while it appears an error to fix
any limitation to the productions of Machinery, Science and Taste which
are of no country, but belong to the Civilised World, particular advantage
to British industry might be derived from placing it in fair competition
with that of other Nations'.

The concept of competition through trade had already been there in the
eighteenth century and earlier, though it had been associated then with
profit and power. By 1851 Europe had enjoyed a period of peace – with
local exceptions on the periphery – which had lasted since 1815. This was
in sharp contrast to eighteenth-century experience when there were
frequent wars, and to early-nineteenth-century experience when Britain
and Europe were still involved in the protracted struggles which followed
the French Revolution and the rise of Napoleon. War undoubtedly gave a
stimulus to the iron industry – armaments production was a major
constituent of iron output, and there were problems in peacetime after

1860, when pots, pans and pipes had to take the place of guns – yet it made the development of that industry jerky and inefficient. Wars also directly stimulated the production of timber, copper, lead, leather and chemicals, even of coarse grades of woollen cloth. Indirectly, it helped a few consumer industries, like silk: the Spitalfields silk industry thrived most during the Napoleonic Wars when it was protected against the French. Yet war meant that the cotton industry was disturbed, that overseas markets were in jeopardy, that there was a diversion of effort from houses, workshops and certain branches of transport. It was associated, too, with financial fluctuations and with price rises which limited consumption. The Revolutionary and Napoleonic Wars are calculated to have cost Britain £1,000 million in direct military expenditure. When Thackeray wrote of 'bloodless weapons' in his 1851 ode, he was drawing a contrast, soon to be sharpened in the mid-1850s by the Crimean War.

The fact that the triumph of civil engineering had long surpassed military and naval engineering by 1851 was brought out in the Crystal Palace building itself. Brunel had hoped in 1849 that the Exhibition building might become the most important exhibit in the Exhibition: 'I believe that there is no one object to be exhibited so *peculiarly* fitted for competition as the design and construction of the vast building itself. Skill of construction, economy of construction and rapidity of construction would call forth all those resources for which England is distinguished. I believe it might be much the grandest subject of competition of the whole affair.'

As it was, William Cubitt, Chairman of the Building Committee, and his colleagues who included Brunel and Stephenson as well as the Duke of Buccleuch (himself an engineer), chose in Paxton a gardener rather than an engineer – albeit a very special kind of gardener. Moreover, Paxton's dominating conception, a palace of glass and iron, was the conservatory which he had built for the Duke of Devonshire at Chatsworth, a special building to house not machinery but a very special kind of water-lily brought from South America, and named *Victoria regia*, which flowered in its new home for the first time in 1849 and quickly outgrew its tank. Paxton had been designing glass structures for more than twenty years – he had written an article about them in 1835 in the *Magazine for Botany* – and he had also been very heavily involved in railway planning and speculation. In 1865, his obituary in *The Times* described him as 'the founder of a new style of architecture'. Yet there is a curious kind of associational link with Darwin's *Botanical Garden* (the plant inspired the structure) and with some of the great railway sheds and stations – Bristol's Temple Meads Station (1835–40), for example, had a wooden false hammer-beam roof with a clear span of 72 ft. One of the other entries for the 1851 competition was from Richard Turner who had designed both the Palm House in Kew Gardens (1844) and the great train-shed at Lime Street Station in Liverpool (1845–57).

The novelty of Paxton's plan lay not only in its conception but in its implementation. It was a building which could not have been erected even fifty years earlier. Interchangeable parts had to be employed – the product of the machine-tool industry – and plate glass had to be available in huge quantities. (It came from Chance Brothers at Smethwick, though Dickens's *Household Words* pointed out in the same year that in one week the employees of the Thames Plate Glass Works were turning out as much plate glass after the ending of the excise duty in 1845 as all the glass-workers in the country put together before.) The method of building was modular – prefabrication was essential – and it was machines which turned out the sash-bars and gutters and laid on the paint. The structure relied for its lateral stability entirely on the rigid connection between vertical iron columns and horizontal beams, in this way being distinguished from the great train-sheds.

Hopes that the Great Exhibition would engender a 'new architecture' were no more realized than hopes that it would perpetuate peace, although in 1849 French writers had been arguing that the new architecture would be architecture in iron, and in 1858 George Gilbert Scott, protagonist of Gothic though he was, argued in his *Remarks on Secular and Domestic Architecture* that it was 'self-evident' that 'the triumph of modern metallic construction opens out a perfectly new field for architectural development'. It was only with the development of the American skyscraper that 'new architecture' emerged, based on the steel frame, and it was only *after* this development that the full significance of the Crystal Palace in the history of architecture has come to be appreciated, as it is in Sigfried Giedion's *Space, Time and Architecture* (1941). Giedion's pages on the use of iron start with Darby, Fairbairn, Stephenson and Telford and encompass cotton-mills (including Philip and Lee's Saltaire Mill of 1851) and the Britannia Bridge, as well as several French buildings and American engineers, notably James Bogardus (1800–74). A period of slightly more than eight decades, he points out, spanned the first iron-columned fireproof mill and the first iron-framed American skyscraper, and he quotes the famous comment of Le Corbusier in 1924 that 'the century of the machine awakened the architect. New tastes and new possibilities produced him.'

There were certainly lags in the process, which should not be conceived as a linear one, mainly, perhaps, as Giedion suggests, because of the separation of the architect from the engineer. Yet there were lags, too, in the process of producing well-designed objects which would meet the daily requirements of the consumer. The eighteenth century had produced many beautiful things. Taste was assured, though it was the taste of a growing minority. Pottery, for example, was deliberately produced to vie with that of France: 'I am fully satisfied with your reasons for the *Virtuosi* of France being fond of *Elegant Simplicity*', Wedgwood wrote to his partner Thomas Bentley in 1769, 'and shall more than ever make that idea a leading principle in my useful, as well as our Ornamental works.' 'We think so much alike about flowers being allways stuck in the wrong place,' he went on, that 'No more flowers was one of my first orders when I came home.' The same canons influenced Adam's fireplaces and attitudes towards interior decoration – Thomas Hope produced his *Household Furniture and Interior Decoration* in 1807, said to be the first book on interior decoration – and while furniture could have its elements of fantasy and there was more than one style, Sheraton's – 'almost fragile in its lightness' – is said to have been 'technically perfect'. Of eighteenth-century costume James Laver has written that there seems to be a 'unity', 'the mark of a civilized life'.

Behind the scenes, however, there were new forces at work, particularly pressures to expand markets. One reason why Sheraton furniture was so light was that manufacturers were trying to cut costs and to economize in wood. Wedgwood's sensitivity to markets was apparent at every stage of his career: 'I have had several serious *Talks* with men at the Ornamental works lately about the price of our workmanship, and the necessity of lowering it,' he wrote in 1772. 'Middling people' would then buy more. The desire to produce cheaper products was one of the incentives behind the growth of machine production. But the desire for greater ostentation in products and for a wider range of styles was a second, apparently independent force. The 'economy of delight', as J. U. Nef has called it, was not to rest for ever on the late eighteenth-century balance. Chippendale used Chinese and Gothic styles. Ex-revolutionaries in Paris turned to the ornate pomp of the Empire. Not all the post-war arts were 'polite'. By 1840 Sir Francis Palgrave (1788–1861) was claiming that 'one of the results of machinery' was 'a permanent glut of pseudo-art'.

It would not be correct, therefore, to draw a sharp contrast between eighteenth-century products and Victorian products. The intervening period, which included both the Brighton Pavilion and the retreat from Brighton, must be taken into the reckoning. In one respect Palgrave was wrong. 'Art can never again take root in the affections of mankind', he wrote. Eleven years later, the Great Exhibition proved him wrong, although it proved perhaps also that 'affections' are not enough.

There was certainly no shortage of objects in 1851. Quantity prevailed. This was 'the great Victorian collection', and the way in which the objects were classified and catalogued in 1851 is itself revealing. There were six major sections – raw materials; machinery; manufactures – textile fabrics; manufactures – metallic, vitreous and ceramic; miscellaneous; and fine arts. Within this simple system there were no less than thirty 'classes', however, beginning with Class I – 'Mining, Quarrying, Metallurgical Operations and Mineral Products', and ending with Class XXX – 'Sculpture, Models (in Architecture, Topography and Anatomy) and Plastic Art'. All other fine arts, as such, were excluded.

The title of Class V, 'Machines for direct use, including Carriages and Railway and Naval Mechanisms', implied that there were many machines which were not in direct use. It was on the acquisition and use of these, indeed, that much English capital was deployed. Prince Albert had made a fundamental error in suggesting initially a division of objects into three sections – the raw materials of industry; the manufactures made from them; and 'the art used to adorn them'; and Karl Marx was nearer to appreciating what the intermediate machines meant. 'Production gives consumption its specificity,' he stated in his *Grundrisse* notebooks (1857/8). Yet as the process of production becomes more complex, some of the products used in the process disappear altogether, the workers provide mere 'linkages', and 'the machines themselves, including the intermediate machines, count.' 'Nature builds no machines, no locomotives, railways, electric telegraphs, self-acting mules, etc. these are products of human industry: natural material transformed into organs of the human will.' Marx singled out the achievement of Richard Roberts: 'What has Vulcan against Roberts & Co.?' 'All mythology overcomes and dominates and shapes the forces of nature in the imagination and by the imagination: it therefore vanishes with the advent of real mastery over them. What becomes of *Fama* alongside Printing House Square?'

Machine tools brought out this point most clearly in 1851, for at that time they were far more intelligently and carefully conceived than either the final products (only a limited range of which were destined for the ordinary consumer) or the raw materials (whose chemistry was little understood and for which there were few synthetic substitutes). Dr Lyon Playfair, the young scientist who was 'Special Commissioner to Communicate with Local Committees', fully appreciated this, and he must have been delighted that the public took almost as much interest in Whitworth's display of machine tools – he had twenty-three exhibits – as it did in the locomotives.

In his *A History of Machine Tools* (1969), W. Steeds does not single out the Exhibition as a landmark, although he describes their evolution from 1750 to 1910. Few machine tools, he says, have survived from the eighteenth century, but many do from the period 1800 to 1830 (one example, Henry Maudslay's 1810 lathe, made for sale rather than use and costing £200, is on display in the Science Museum). Among the 1851 objects were a diminutive machine 'made for the use of opticians', a railway-wheel lathe, and, in the Queen's phrase, a shearing and punching machine for iron 'of just $\frac{1}{2}$ an inch thick, doing it as if it were bread!'

One whole class (XI) of objects was devoted to cotton and one (XXII) to iron and general hardware, and 'agricultural and horticultural machines and implements' were treated as Class IX. The textiles exhibits included a huge Jacquard loom, first invented by J.M. Jacquard (1752–1834) and first applied in Britain to the silk industry. The agricultural exhibits included several from the United States (see below, p. 177), portents of the future. In the section devoted to civil engineering there was a model of the Liverpool Docks, complete with 1,600 rigged ships, and among the locomotives there was the giant *Liverpool*, built to the design of Thomas Crompton by Bury, Curtis and Kennedy, and Daniel Gooch's even bigger, 31-ton *Lord of the Isles*, built for the broad-gauge Great Western Railway.

Between the *Rocket* and the *Liverpool* and the *Lord of the Isles* there had been some famous locomotives. The *Derwent*, built by Alfred Kitchen – a six-coupled goods engine – now stands on a pedestal in Darlington Station. Gooch, born in the North-East in the shadow of the ironworks that produced the wrought-iron rails for the Stockton and Darlington, had become Locomotive Assistant to Brunel on the Great Western in 1837 and had produced many engines for him after Brunel had bought from Stephenson the *North Star* ('a splendid engine . . . it would have been a beautiful ornament in the most elegant drawing-room'). Gooch's *Firefly* (1840) was of a new design, the first of sixty-two similar locomotives, among them the *Actæon* which first did the long journey from Paddington to Exeter non-stop in 1844, an achievement described by O.S. Nock in his book *The Railway Engineers* (1955) as 'the most spectacular locomotive performance the world had ever witnessed'. Meanwhile, Stephenson was producing 'long-boilered' engines, of which the *Richmond* was an early type (after a mishap in 1849 the cylinders were reduced in size). The *White Horse of Kent* was used in the preparations for the gauge trials of 1845 which began with the victory of Gooch's *Ixion* over Stephenson's *The Great A*. The record of the *Ixion* was subsequently beaten by Gooch's *The Great Western*. Given the victory of the narrower Stephenson gauge, Rolt is right to compare the Gooch/Brunel exploits with Prince Rupert's cavalry charges in the seventeenth-century war between Charles I and Parliament.

However great the appeal of the locomotive section in 1851, it was the wide range of objects on display (many of them carried by locomotive) which was the main appeal. 'Electric machines' were left out on grounds advanced by Brunel that they were mere 'toys'. But there was a special place for the world of paper products which was beginning to be as visible as the world of glass. There were books on display – not least the *Official Description* with a frontispiece designed by John Tenniel – as well as machines concerned with paper and printing, and there was an impressive De La Rue exhibit, including an envelope-making machine which produced 2,700 envelopes an hour. It drew enormous crowds: 'none other can boast of bigger congregations', wrote the *Illustrated London News*. 'There are few things in fact which Paxton's glass shade contains more attractive to the curious than this.' A firm of London tailors inserted an advertisement in the *Morning Herald* of 6 June 1851 headed 'The Expanding Figure of the Great Exhibition', by which it meant the machine. And it added – with an eye to the future – that 'however successful this invention may prove, in measurement it will after all be "measure for measure" when placed in comparison with the fit of our own durable, well made, fashionable and cheap specimens of gentlemen's attire.'

The age of cheap ready-made clothes had not yet come. But there were two other 'objects' which had. In 1840 Britain had introduced the world's first adhesive postage stamps, and although De La Rue's were not yet making them, penny stamps were doubtless being affixed in 1851 to many letters describing the Exhibition. (Postcards had not yet been introduced, although Cole had pioneered the Christmas card.) Some of the letters must have been written with the new steel pens on display at the Exhibition. These had first been produced in large numbers in 1828. Only one object foretold the possible end of the age of paper – the electric telegraph. It was introduced to keep the Exhibition officials in touch with the Police. Yet it delighted the Queen. 'It is the most wonderful thing,' she wrote, 'and the boy who works it does so with the greatest ease and rapidity.'

The Queen, one of the 6 million visitors to the Exhibition – and a very regular one, was in general impressed less by the bazaar-like aspect of it all than by 'the effect of fairyland'. She liked seeing the Swiss watches and musical boxes, the Aubusson tapestries, the Turkish silks, a medal-making machine which produced fifty medals a minute, and the wood-carving (including her own family's 'wonderful cradle'), but she also studied far more machinery than any previous monarch. 'Some of the inventions', she remarked, 'were very ingenious, many of them quite Utopian.' The Exhibition, she concluded, 'has taught me so much I never knew before – has brought me in contact with so many clever people I should never have known otherwise, and with so many manufacturers whom I would scarcely have met unless I travelled all over the country and visited every individual manufactory which I never could have done. At the Exhibition everything is brought together in a small space and one has all the advantages of seeing the different exhibits together.'

Contrasts have often been drawn between the engineering exhibits in the Great Exhibition and the objects in the galleries devoted to the arts and to domestic life. The former, according to L. T. C. Rolt, shared with the building which housed them 'a clear functional beauty of line and proportion unmarred by any excess', while the latter resembled 'some vast lumber room where a jetsam of miscellaneous objects, some pathetic, some ludicrous, but all representing a prodigal misuse of labour and ingenuity, lie gathering dust'.

It is, perhaps, too easy a contrast, and it needs to be expanded and explained as well as presented. As machines became more specialized, all kinds of effects could be achieved that had not been possible before. As Gottfried Semper (1803–79), an enlightened German architect critic of the Exhibition put it, 'the machine sews, knits, embroiders, carves, paints and . . . puts to shame all human skill'. Inevitably its initial exploitation led to 'confusions', particularly when it was in the hands of 'speculators' anxious to make quick profits from customers who had had no education in taste. Nikolaus Pevsner puts matters in perspective in his *High Victorian Design* (1931), where he describes 'the buoyancy and showiness of so much at the Crystal Palace' as 'the final flourish of a century of great commercial expansion. Hence the amplitude and lavishness of the style, and hence the indiscriminate faith in novelty and tricky gadgets.'

Eighteenth-century taste had for more than a decade been thought to be 'dull' and 'monotonous', like Chippendale furniture or Adam fireplaces or the town of Bath, 'long rows of shops and houses . . . tortured into strict uniformity, exactly of the same height'. What was in demand was variety. There was not one canon of taste, although there were, of course, several influential contemporaries (Pugin with his belief in Gothic was one: Ruskin was another) who continued to insist that there was. All styles should be made accessible and, if thought desirable, copied. Curves were preferred to straight lines, decoration to plainness of surface. Even engineering exhibits – and certainly mills, as we have seen, and manufactured products – could be 'ornamental', made ornamental, indeed, to Ruskin's horror, by machine. So, too, could and were the materials of the industrial revolution. A table or a statue might be made out of zinc or a garden seat out of a block of coal. Granite could be cut like chalk, and inferior materials could increasingly easily be covered by superior ones. There was ample room for what Ruskin called 'deceits'. In less than ten years from 1837 to 1846 the Patent Office granted thirty-five patents for the 'coating and covering of non-metallic bodies'. The dipping process became almost as important in relation to products as the rolling process had been in relation to machines (see above, p. 140). Electroplating is merely one of the best examples. And papier mâché, pressed and moulded paper pulp, produced by another novel process, was a characteristic product, much in demand for a wide range of products.

If materials could be treated so freely, why not designs, too? There were 'battles' here, with Cole and his remarkable *Journal of Design* (1849–52), the first journal to deal exclusively with industrial design, protesting against the florid and the archaic – wallpapers and carpets with huge brightly coloured flowers and fruit (Dickens dealt with this theme in the brilliant opening chapter of *Hard Times*, published in 1854) or match-boxes in Parian porcelain or in ormolu designed to look like Crusaders' tombs (even though the boxes in Parian porcelain were made by Minton, Cole's favourite firm). 'Make your carpet a background for setting your furniture appropriately and well.' As for novelties, 'Heaven and earth and the wide sea cannot obtain the forms and fancies that are here displayed . . . like the whimsies of madness.' *The Times* was on Cole's side. In an article entitled 'Universal Infidelity in Principles of Design' it complained that 'the absence of any fixed principles in ornamental design is apparent in the

Exhibition. . . . It seems to us that the art manufacturers of the whole of Europe are thoroughly demoralised.' A.W.N. Pugin would have agreed. There was one style as there was one God.

William Morris (1834–96), too, could be equally scathing – and he would have been tougher with Cole than Pugin was. When he went to the Great Exhibition he refused to go round and look at the exhibits, declaring it all 'wonderfully ugly'. Yet there were awkwardnesses in Pugin's, in Morris's and Ruskin's own approaches to materials and designs. Pugin was happy to make functionally awkward stoves in Gothic, though he always stressed the importance of the functional. Ruskin refused to believe that iron was a suitable material for construction and compared railway stations ('alien to architecture') with rat-holes and wasps' nests, and Morris disliked plate-glass windows because they let in too much light and dismissed 'modern engineering as a horrible and restless nightmare'.

Another visitor to the Exhibition, William Whiteley, three years older than Morris, was by contrast so moved by the Exhibition that he began to dream of large retail stores, 'universal providers', shops with plate-glass fronts. The bazaar would become permanent. The result was a highly successful retail business, although it was not until 1872 that Whiteley began to call himself the universal provider. Retailing was relatively slow to develop, and it was not until after the Great Exhibition that the department store emerged as a distinct kind of enterprise: Aristide Boucicault started his Bon Marché one year later in 1852. For decades, however, there had been covered markets. Liverpool had one in 1822 which was said to be 'far bigger and more imposing than the Halles in Paris'. Itinerant retailing was in decline by 1851, though London street cries (like 'All a-blowing, all a-growing') could still be heard. The number of shops including 'general shops', was increasing, and so, too, was the range of products which could be bought there. Advertising was closely related to showmanship, and many products which in the late nineteenth century were 'branded' were still being sold straight from the warehouse.

Little attention was paid at the Great Exhibition to the cost of cleaning, handling or storing the products on display, none of which was priced: the exhibits predicated plentiful domestic service and the draughty spaces of the Victorian home. There was an increasing emphasis, however, on comfort, although A.J. Downing could describe an American easy chair in 1850 as a 'lounge better adapted for siesta than to promote the grace or dignity of the figure'. The furniture section, according to one contemporary, was evidence more than any other of 'our national prosperity'. 'The contributions to this section included every species of decoration, for churches, for palaces, for private dwellings, upholstery and paper hangings, japanned goods and papier mâché.' There was an air of solidarity in the mahogany, even of permanence. Yet the commentator had one regret: 'Amidst all the ornamental works in furniture . . . there were to be found so few specimens of ordinary furniture in general use. . . .'

In a section on 'consumption' in the 1851 edition of G.R. Porter's *The Progress of the Nation*, the author referred in particular to the improvement in the dwellings of the middle classes. 'It is not necessary to go back much beyond half a century to arrive at the time when prosperous shopkeepers in the leading thoroughfares of London were without that necessary article of furniture, a carpet, in their sitting-rooms. . . . In the same houses we now see not carpets merely, but many articles of furniture which were formerly

The Model House for working-class families, designed by Henry Roberts at the request of Prince Albert and erected as a showplace in Hyde Park at the time of the Great Exhibition.

in use only among the nobility and gentry'. Porter might have added gas-lighting to the comforts. Incandescent burners were not introduced until 1879, but already the gentle purring sound made by gas as it emerged from the flame-holder is said to have added to the sense of well-being.

There were, of course, far more uncomfortable homes in 1851 than there were comfortable ones. The debate about working-class standards of living during the years of early industrialization continues, but whatever improvements there had been were limited. It is interesting to note that average consumption of sugar rose from 19·94 lb per person in 1830 to 24·12 lb per person in 1849, though the lowest annual *per capita* consumption figure (15·28 lb) came half-way through the period in 1840, in a year of high sugar prices and economic depression. Meanwhile, tea consumption increased greatly after a reduction of duty in 1841: total quantities were 37,355,911 lb in 1842 and 50,021,576 lb in 1849. As for house and home themselves, there was one very special object on display – not in the Exhibition itself but near by on vacant land near Knightsbridge Barracks. Prince Albert's Model Lodging House, built in hollow brick, was designed to house four working-class families. Each dwelling was entered through a small lobby. Each had a living-room; a scullery fitted with sink, coal-bin, plate-rack, meat-safe, fitted shelves and dresser-flap; and three bedrooms to provide for 'that separation which, with a family, is so essential to morality and decency'.

Each dwelling, too, had a Staffordshire glazed water-closet; and this as much as any other fixture – and it must have been the envy of some middle-class families in 1851 – was more a sign of the times even than the furniture. There were towns where the water-supply was appalling, and there were thousands of working-class houses with only the most primitive sanitation. Yet it did not need Edwin Chadwick to explain how important this invention was. To round off two centuries, it is interesting to turn to a letter of March 1775 in which Josiah Wedgwood discussed cisterns for water-closets with his cousin. 'The sale for them will in all probability be very considerable,' he wrote. Purchasers 'now give nine or ten guineas for Marble Cisterns and do not order those of our ware for the cheapest . . . but they will be sweeter than the Marble ones. . . . Make them one inch thick or more if you please, for the Architects do not care how thick they are.'

While the design of household objects brought out fundamental differences between the eighteenth and nineteenth centuries, there were continuing economic and social tendencies across both centuries – the desire for material betterment 'on the demand side' and the pressure to widen markets and to reduce prices on 'the supply side'. Soap output charged with duty stood, for example, at 28.6 million lb in 1750, 36·5 million lb in 1780, 49·3 million lb in 1800, 105·8 million lb in 1830, and 173 million lb in 1850. *Per capita* consumption was increasing steadily, therefore, in a period of rapidly rising population – and that despite excise control and heavy duties which were sharply raised in 1816 to 3*d* per lb on hard soap.

Such regressive indirect taxation, which was the basis of Government finance until Peel brought back income tax in 1842, had bad social consequences. As the *Penny Cyclopaedia*, published by the Society for the Diffusion of Useful Knowledge, stated bluntly in 1841, a subsequent reduction of duty by a half 'has not only been successful as a financial measure, but has conferred the greatest benefit on the poorer classes who now consume a better and therefore more economical soap than before.' 'The old duty of 3*d* per lb discouraged cleanliness and led to disease and its attendant evils.'

There were no taxes on cotton, and cotton goods were lighter and more easily washable than those made of wool or linen. Cotton calicoes, 'print goods', had become the staple material for working-class women's dresses long before 1851, while their husbands or fathers wore cotton shirts and fustian trousers and jackets. Wool and silk were favoured by those middle-class families with income to spare and by the aristocracy – and clothes were made up for them by an over-worked labour force of seamstresses and milliners, whose conditions of work were often worse than those in the mills. (There were 268,000 milliners and dressmakers at the time of the 1851 Census, as against 502,000 people working in cotton calico *134* manufacture, including printing and dyeing.) That fustian could become a class symbol was proved when Feargus O'Connor deliberately addressed Chartist crowds in a fustian suit.

On the other side of the Atlantic class differences were less marked, and the American exhibits at the Crystal Palace received much attention for this and other reasons. *The Times* noted 'several very interesting machines' in the American section and praised the 'useful character of the display' as contrasted with the 'showy' exhibits in some of the other national sections, while the *Illustrated London News* reported that visitors were switching their interest as the Exhibition proceeded from the European to the American displays.

XV   It is true that a huge sculpture of an eagle – America's national symbol – dominated the display, which included a bar of soap used by Jenny Lind (along with many other soaps, some in the form of flowers and letters, and dentifrices and tooth-washers) and ice-making machines (not to speak of corn-husk mattresses). Yet the exhibits which really counted were a Cyrus McCormick reaper (of great importance in farm development), a sewing-machine (such machines were to transform dressmaking), a prize-winning Hobbs lock (Hobbs successfully picked two 'secure' British locks, including the Bramah lock), and a wide range of Colt revolvers (like the locks a triumph of standardization). The small sewing-machine from New York, already used in the making not of fancy dresses but of socks and pantaloons, could be worked by one girl turning 600 stitches a minute, but the full potential of the sewing-machine was not fully realized in 1851. By contrast, even at the time Dickinson's two-volume *Comprehensive Pictures of the Great Exhibition* (1854) could state simply but prophetically of the McCormick reaper that 'in agriculture it appears that the machine will be as important as the spinning-jenny and the mule'.

Of the American exhibits as a whole, C.T. Rodgers, the author of *American Supremacy at the World's Fair* (Philadelphia, 1852), could claim that 'they made the Yankee chest swell a little.' 'To Americanise British land and sea machinery would half revolutionize Britain.' 'Our pieces are adapted to a larger theatre.' 'Our instruments are made to act where wider elbow room and less labor are afforded.' 'For the magnitude of our enterprises,' Rodgers went on, 'John Bull has more wonder than sympathy.' This was an optimistic American verdict. Horace Greeley of the *New York Tribune*, one of the American Commissioners, was more cautious. 'Our share in the Exhibition was creditable to us as a nation not a century old . . . but it fell far short of what it might have been and did not fairly exhibit the progress and present condition of the Useful Arts in this country. We can and must do better next time.'

Next time came soon, for there were other international Exhibitions in the mid-century years, but the real American response came when the United States was a century old in 1876. The idea of a Centennial Exhibition was conceived at the Smithsonian Institution in 1864. Yet, although three years later Secretary of State Seward wrote of exhibitions as a whole that 'they advance human knowledge in all directions' and were becoming 'national necessities and duties', there was as much difficulty in sponsoring and planning the Centennial as there had been in sponsoring and planning the Exhibition of 1851. If much of the spirit of 1851 suggested Samuel Smiles, much of the progress of 1876, as Robert C. Post has written, resembled a popular story by Horatius Alger – poor beginnings, large obstacles, but obstacles overcome by hard work. That both were eventually huge successes was a tribute not only to the imagination and the ingenuity of the planners and exhibitors, but the the curiosity and sociability of the visitors, themselves ultimately the clients and customers. And both exhibitions were to inspire centennials of their own – the Festival of Britain in 1951 and the Washington Revival Exhibition of 1976.

McCormick's reaping machine, one of the important developments in agriculture was on show at the Great Exhibition.

The Great Exhibition

160 Joseph Paxton's design for the Crystal Palace was significant for its use of standardized prefabricated elements: an engraving published in *The Expositor* in December 1850 shows the preparations for hoisting the roof ribs of the transept into place.

161, 162 The idea of the Great Exhibition as the world's first trade fair is epitomized in an etching by George Cruikshank, as is the scale of the display areas in a view looking down the main avenue. The building was 1,848 ft long and 456 ft across at its widest point.

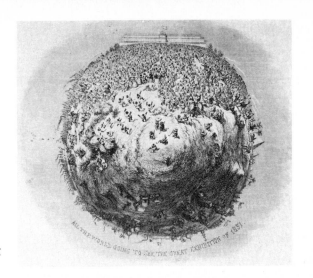

163 *Left*. Prince Albert's season ticket was No. 1 of a total of 773,766 issued to cover the 141 days on which the exhibition was open. The total number of visitors exceeded six million.

164 The cast-iron gates, made at Coalbrookdale, which adorned the entrance to the North Transept of the Crystal Palace, can still be seen today; they now divide Hyde Park from Kensington Gardens, not far from their original site.

165–167 *Opposite*. Among the works illustrated in the Exhibition Jury Reports published in 1852 were: (above, left) the Crystal Fountain (27 ft high) by F. & C. Osler, which stood at the centre point of the building; (above, right) a hydraulic turbine from France built by Fromont & Son of Chartres, which was awarded a Council Medal; and cast-iron fire-surrounds by Hoole, Robson & Hoole.

168–170 The Machinery Court at the Great
Exhibition included the powerful hydraulic press
which had been employed in raising the tubes of the
Britannia Bridge (cf. *ill. 113*). Among the useful and
ornamental objects shown by the Coalbrookdale
Company was a cast-iron fountain, 7 ft 6 in. in height
(above, right); and the same company also produced
ornate pillars for street lighting – this example on the
south side of Trafalgar Square in London was
illustrated in one of the company's catalogues.

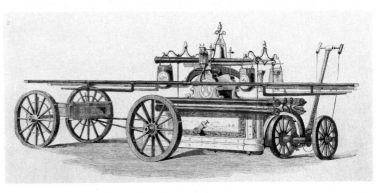

171, 172 Among the machines developed in North America at the time of the Great Exhibition were a gold-winnowing device from California and a hand-operated fire-pump from Montreal which was shown in 1851.

173 The aftermath of the Great Exhibition, as depicted in another etching by George Cruikshank (cf. *ill. 161*); the official closing ceremony (cf. *colour plate XVI*) took place on 15 October 1851.

Other exhibitions

174–176 The success of the 1851
Exhibition spawned several other
schemes of a similar nature, among
the earliest being: (left) the interior –
very similar to that of the Crystal
Palace – of the New York Exhibition
of 1853; (below) the 'Palais de
l'Industrie' at the Paris Exhibition of
1855, where a huge sheet of plate glass
was prominently displayed; and
(opposite) the foreign nave, seen from
the western dome, of the 1862
exhibition at South Kensington (the
buildings were later transferred to
North London, and destroyed by fire –
as was the Crystal Palace long after its
transfer to Sydenham.

Distribution

177, 178 The French exhibits destined for the Crystal Palace were dispatched by train from Paris in March 1851. The use of rails for transporting heavy goods could also be adapted (below) to warehouse handling situations, such as the Pickford's depot, designed by Lewis Cubitt, at Camden Town.

179, 180 With the coming of a countrywide network of railways in the United States, the way was open for trading by mail-order firms operating from a large central headquarters: the checking and invoicing of individual orders at Montgomery Ward & Co. (founded in 1872) is shown in an engraving of 1878, with (below) the cover of the Sears, Roebuck catalogue for 1897.

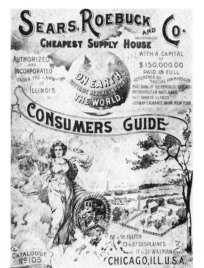

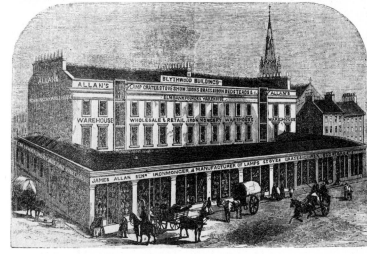

181 The increase in city populations created a demand for consumer products: the variety of choice offered by a large specialist establishment is suggested in an engraving showing an ironmongery warehouse in Glasgow.

182, 183 The bustle of activity
associated with ships and shipbuilding
on the Clyde in 1878 reflects the
important role of the steamship in
international trade. On the other side
of the Atlantic bales of cotton began
their journey down the Mississippi to
the port of New Orleans on a paddle-
steamer, the loading in this case being
aided by the use of a specially
constructed chute.

6 Epilogue

WHATEVER the degree of Britain's industrial supremacy at the time of the Great Exhibition, doubts were already being expressed as to whether it could be maintained. There is 'a certain degree of timidity' among English mechanics, James Nasmyth wrote three years after the Exhibition, 'resulting from traditional notions and attachment to old systems'. And an American commentator in 1851 itself noted how 'English overseers are trained too much to one thing or machine and do not *adapt* themselves readily to circumstances – finding everything wrong which they have not been accustomed to.'

It is tempting to trace back Britain's twentieth-century problems to the prevalence of obsolete attitudes rather than of obsolete machinery. Yet in the long run resources were relevant, too. The people of the United States have been described as 'the people of plenty', and during the last decades of the nineteenth century they were able to make use of huge coal and iron deposits. And as the United States – and Europe – moved from the age of iron into the age of steel mainly after 1870 (when only 10 per cent of Britain's iron output emerged as steel), countries other than Britain were able by this time to exploit a new British process, developed by Thomas and Gilchrist in 1878, far more effectively than Britain itself could. By 1914 Germany, unified in 1871, was producing almost twice as much steel as Britain, and United States was well ahead of both. (The Bessemer converter, the first significant change in steel production, had been introduced in Britain in 1856.) The intricate scientific technology of steel and its alloys (and the Thomas and Gilchrist 'basic' process came out of the rapidly developing world of higher education) made the rough and ready empirical technology of iron seem primitive and cumbrous. In the same way, electrical power was to make steam-power archaic and wasteful, and oil, the possibilities of which were first appreciated in the United States, was to transform the possibilities for coal. *123*

The spectacular development of American industrialization in the decades after 1870 (coinciding as it did with the German industrial revolution) has received more attention from historians than American economic development before the Civil War. Samuel P. Hays's *The Response to Industrialism* (1957) begins, for instance, in 1885. Yet already by 1851 engine-power in the United States outdistanced that of Britain and there were 28,000 miles of railway in North America as compared with only 17,000 in Europe. Before the coming of steam-power and railways there had been an earlier phase of American industrialization, including the development of a textiles industry based on water-power, and rivers and canals. The first Newcomen engine had been exported to the United States as early as 1755, and Boston was illuminated by gas in 1822 and New York a year later. As early as 1810, Pittsburgh could be called 'a large *186* workshop'. 'I heard everywhere the sound of the hammer and anvil', John Melish wrote, while an early nineteenth-century poet could describe the city in language similar to that of his British counterparts:

> Here PITT, compassed by hills and streams around,
> Compactly built within its narrow bound,
> Stands gloomily magnificent in mantling smoke,
> The western workshop, where useful arts convoke;
> Here chiming hammer and loud puffing steam,
> The rattling dray and the thundering team;
> A bustling crowd with hurried pace,
> And oft' brown industry's sooty face
> Are seen and heard throughout the busy place.

If Pittsburgh, one of a group of towns settled within a generation, was already being compared with Birmingham (Birmingham, Alabama, was a product of the late nineteenth century), there was already an American Manchester, and soon there were clusters of textile towns like Lowell and Holyoke. There were inventors, too, like Oliver Evans, experimenting with steam-engines which had no condenser.

Pittsburgh's output of iron products in 1815, when its settled population was still under 10,000, represented a fourteenfold increase in a period of twelve years. Meanwhile, Cincinnati had a huge steam-powered mill, built on the banks of the Mississippi, half of which was used to grind flour (700 barrels a week) and the other half for woollen manufacture. 'It was much the largest building I had ever seen,' one inhabitant reminisced long after it was destroyed by fire in 1823. By then the steamboat (introduced in 1812) had speeded the movement of commerce. Experiments had taken place on the Potomac as early as 1787, and twenty years later Robert Fulton's *Clermont* travelled up the Hudson River from New York to Albany. Fulton could write to a friend in 1812, 'the Mississippi is conquered', adding modestly that the conquest was 'perhaps as valuable' as that at Jena. 'The invention of the steamboat was intended for us', wrote the editor of the *Cincinnati Gazette*, while in 1829 another local writer added that its coming 'has enabled us to anticipate a state of things which, in the ordinary course of events, it would have required a century to produce. The art of printing scarcely surpassed it in beneficial consequences.'

The textile towns of Massachusetts and New Hampshire, like Manchester, Lowell and Holyoke, had much in common with English textile towns, the last being developed near 'Canal Village', where there were locks for river boats carrying freight north or south. There were bog-ironworks near by and later (by 1827) a 'hydraulic cement manufacture'. 'A spectator standing a quarter of a mile below the fall', Timothy Dwight wrote in 1821, 'is presented with the singular prospect of . . . a sawmill, forge etc. . . . In the river itself and on the shores, the numerous wharves, boats, fishermen and spectators . . . impress on the mind very sprightly ideas of bustle and business.'

American urban historians and labour historians have recently studied in detail the making of the textile communities. Constance Green's *Holyoke, Massachussetts* (1939) led the way, and recently demographers and anthropologists have followed, while American historians of ideas and cultures have examined the influence of 'the machine in the garden'. Contemporaries were usually willing to salute – or occasionally to condemn – the general process of industrialization at least as eloquently as English writers with very similar imagery and turns of phrase; and Professor Richard Wade, who was to go on to write of Chicago and collect a fascinating series of its images, prefaced his stimulating monograph *The Urban Frontier* (1959) with lines of Jonathan Meigs written as early as 1797:

> Where late the savage, hid in ambush, lay,
> Or roamed the uncultured valleys for his prey,
> Her hardy gifts rough Industry extends,
> The graves bow down, the lofty forest bends,
> And see the spires of towns and cities rise,
> And domes and temples swell unto the skies.

The process, however, was uneven, and there were years of depression – after the end of the 1812 War with England, for example, which had stimulated industry (cheaper British goods poured in after 1816), and twenty years later, when a directly related depression hit Britain. It was in the good years, of course, that the lyrical note was strongest. 'The stranger views . . . with wonder the rapidity with which cities sprang up in the forests; and with which barbarism retreats before the approach of art and civilization.'

By the middle years of the nineteenth century, another lyrical theme in industrial history was the incipient internationalism of the processes. Industry – and communications, the children of industry – would unify the world, and engineers would be in the vanguard. The telegraph, which would provide a network for the world, had been invented – appropriately enough – by different people in different countries working independently. There were only 2,000 miles of line in Europe in 1849, but by 1854 there were 15,000 and the Dover–Calais link was opened in the year of the Great Exhibition itself. The merits both of industry and of engineers had already been sung by the Saint-Simonians, the early French socialists who did much to spotlight both the problems and opportunities of an 'industrial society', but the rhetoric was not specifically 'socialist'. 'As commerce, education, and the rapid transition of thought and matter, by telegraph and steam have changed everything,' President Ulysses S. Grant told Congress in his Inaugural Speech of 1873, 'I rather believe that the Great Maker is preparing the world to become one nation, speaking one language, a consummation which will render armies and navies no longer necessary.'

Whatever 'the great Maker' was preparing, men and women were going their own ways – creating lively enterprises, but also segregating the social classes, building huge new cities but leaving slums within them, and all the time relying more and more on machines. Everywhere there were similar patterns. Yet there were diversities of tradition and of social, economic, political and legal structures. European industrialization in consequence was a complex and protracted process which involved what came to be called rather misleadingly a 'sequence' of 'industrial revolutions', the earliest of which took place in Belgium and the most dramatic of which took place in unified Germany after 1870. The first Newcomen engine on the Continent had been erected at Liège as early as 1720/21, seventy years before Germany succeeded in building an engine, though in 1794 Germany acquired its first cotton-mill using an Arkwright water-frame in a village, appropriately called Kromford, near Düsseldorf. Meanwhile, James Watt described J. C. Périer's Chaillot Works in France 'as a most magnificent and commodious manufactory for steam engines where he executes all the parts exceedingly well'.

It is useful in considering the process of European industrialization to distinguish between what Professor David Landes calls 'responses to endogenous pressures' towards change and reactions to new methods developed in Britain. Taking the process as a whole, it is clear that, however strong the desire at times might have been to emulate Britain's progress, Britain could seldom be taken as a model. Other European countries, unlike Britain, had large peasant populations, and all depended more in the course of industrialization on the role of the State even when the praises of free trade were being sung. In Germany, in particular, State policy after 1870 assisted industrialization, although the lines of change were not mapped out in advance. There was a degree of industrial and financial concentration also which had been missing in Britain. At the same time, it was British experience which was usually singled out – at least until the 1880s. Whatever the differences, Britain had 'led the way'. Marx was only one of a number of nineteenth-century thinkers (John Stuart Mill was another) to argue in the light of that experience that 'the country which is more developed industrially only shows to the less developed the image of its own future'.

The development of industry in continental Europe had owed a great deal to British inventors, businessmen and contractors, although the 'endogenous pressures' had often produced their own responses. Thus, experimental steam-powered ships were being tried out on the River *188* Saône in France in the 1780s, and Alfred Krupp, who was producing high-quality steel at Essen by 1817, put on display at the Great Exhibition in 1851 a block of crucible steel weighing 2,150 kg, the largest ever made. British influence was strong despite prohibitions on the export of machinery, not fully lifted until 1842, and on the emigration of skilled artisans, forbidden until 1825. Thus, John Holker had set up as a textile-manufacturer at Rouen in 1751 and was appointed Inspector-General of Factories, a title which would have been impossible in England. He introduced new cotton machinery to France, as John Kay and his sons had done. During the 1790s three skilled British cotton-workers set up a cotton-mill for K. F. Bernhard at Hartau in Saxony, and English water-frames and mules were introduced into Austria, too, where John Thornton became Manager of the thriving Yarn Manufacturing Company in Potterdorf in 1801. The Cockerill family constructed cotton-mills at Verviers in Belgium and woollen mills at Guben and Grünberg in Germany. Even in Russia, where economic development was associated with military pressures, cotton-mills were built before 1800: the initiative in one case came from a serf turned businessman, E. Grachev, who started a linen-manufacture and calico-printing works at Ivanovo.

There were many transfers of technology, including old and new techniques, in the iron industry and in engineering. Michael Alcock established several ironworks in France and William Wilkinson, who built a new cannon factory in Indret in 1777, and Aaron Manby went on to *187* modernize the Le Creusot Works, introducing steam pumps and engines there. (Boulton and Watt had patented their steam-engine in France in 1777/8.) In Silesia, already more industrialized than most parts of Germany, John Baildon erected two coke-furnaces for the iron industry: he subsequently introduced a rotative steam-engine into the Royal Porcelain Works in Berlin. The Seraing Engineering Works near Liège, managed by one of the Cockerill family, John, was perhaps the most integrated plant in

Europe in the 1830s, producing coal, pig-iron, armaments, steam-engines, and other machinery, including locomotives, and railway track.

Locomotives and railway track were symbols of economic progess everywhere, and Marx found an appealing phrase when he called the railway-builders the light cavalry of capitalism. In this story Britain had certainly taken the lead: it exported 1,291,000 tons of railroad iron and steel in the five years between 1845 and 1849 and as many as 2,846,000 tons in the following five-year period, 1850–54. The benefits were widely diffused. In 1845 there were nine countries in Europe with railways, in 1855 fourteen. Nor was Europe the only continent to benefit. Thomas Brassey (1805–70) – outstanding among the great railway contractors of the nineteenth century – sometimes employed 80,000 men in five continents. By 1855 there were railways in all five of them. They often involved engineering exploits of the highest order, and a whole folklore (and literature) was associated with them. There was even 'a line to Heaven' made by Christ and having 'life Eternal' as its destination.

When these lines were written – and they soon made their way across the Atlantic – Britain was still far ahead of all its competitors. In 1851, indeed, Belgium, the next most intensively developed country, still had half its total working population engaged in agriculture, as against a quarter in Britain. The British cotton industry, which accounted for 46 per cent of Britain's total exports, was equal in size to that of all the other countries in Europe combined. And during the unprecedented boom years of the 1850s Britain held on to its lead even when other countries were industrializing. Indeed, British exports of cotton goods actually increased at a faster rate during that decade than had been achieved during each of the three previous decades.

By the 1860s, however, the gap between Britain and continental Europe was closing, and doubts about the future were being widely expressed, particularly at the time of the Paris Exhibition of 1867. By the 1870s fear of competition was fully justified, and there was soon talk of 'retardation' and 'deceleration'. The German and American economies were advancing by then two or three times faster each year than the British. These were thought of as the two great competitors. 'Sixty years ago, England had a lead in most branches of industry,' Alfred Marshall, the distinguished British economist, wrote in 1908. 'It was inevitable that she could cede much of the leadership to the great land [the United States] which attracts alert minds of all nations to sharpen their inventive and resourceful faculties by impact on one another. It was inevitable that she should yield a little of it to that land of great industrial traditions which yoked science in the service of man with unrivalled energy [Imperial Germany]. It was not inevitable that she should lose so much of it as she has done.'

Questions are still being asked – and answered in different ways – about the inevitability of the loss of leadership – its causes and its implications. 'Did Victorian Britain fail?' 'When was the climacteric?' How is it related to Britain's current economic weakness? What is certain is that as the modes of industrialization changed in an age of steel – and ultimately of electric power, chemicals and scientific research and development – Britain's lead was irrevocably lost . . . and the basic industries of the early industrial revolution – coal, cotton, iron and railways – soon became problem industries. The variables which determine economic growth are many and include psychological and sociological (including educational)

Opposite
184 Art, engineering and idealism were combined in Frédéric Auguste Bartholdi's symbolic 151-ft high Statue of Liberty, presented by the French people to the United States in 1886, but here seen while under construction in Paris, towering above the near-by buildings.

influences, as well as quantities of economic resources and industrial techniques.

As far as the diverse techniques are concerned – and they have been a major theme of this book – it was, significantly, *The Engineer* which wrote in 1901 that 'a hasty acceptance of apparent improvements is to be deprecated. Because a machine has a large output, it does not follow that it must be better economically than one that produces less rapidly. Speed has to be paid for in one way or another.' Few engineers, whether or not they called themselves by that name, would have said the same in 1801. By 1901, American ways of producing were markedly different from those of Britain, as were the products – and the ways of thinking about products and processes. There had always been greater emphasis across the Atlantic on speed than there was in Britain, and there had always been a greater interest in adaptability. American locomotives were being built by the 1850s, for example, 'as loose-jointed as a basket' and capable of 'adjusting the engine to its road at every instant of its journey'; and even earlier 'balloon-frame' houses were being constructed which were hailed by the anonymous writers of *The Great Industries of the United States* in 1873 as 'the most important contribution to our domestic architecture which the spirit of economy, and a scientific adaptation of means to ends have given the modern world.' Standardized machine tools were further examples of adaptability, and as early as 1847 John Platt in Manchester could claim that 'it is the custom among machine makers in England to purchase inventions from the Americans and adapt them to use in this country'. Near the beginning of the century – in 1805 – a writer on architecture in *The New and Complete American Encyclopaedia* had noted 'the facility with which we *may* move' as 'a strong incentive to that love of change' which already characterized Americans. Britain, having changed so rapidly in the great transformation from the 1780s to the 1850s, showed less and less willingness to change in the late-nineteenth and twentieth centuries.

Meanwhile, there have been many twentieth-century 'industrial revolutions' outside Europe, the first in Japan, like Britain an island and small enough in area to have to depend on its exports, and the latest in South Korea not very far away. As the balance of world economic power changes and political as well as social and cultural change continues to be associated with industrialization, experience accumulates and perspectives alter. It is a sign of the times that while newspapers, magazines and television throughout the world spotlight Britain's continuing economic difficulties – and there is no lack of images there – we can also trace a growing interest not only in Britain, but throughout the world, in the heritage of the world's first industrial revolution and the images associated with it.

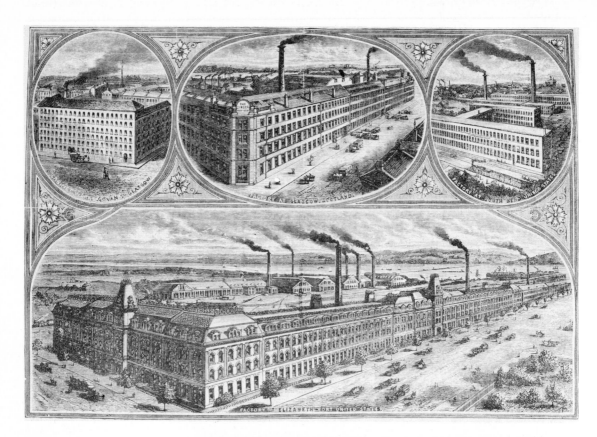

185, 186 The spread of manufacturing and heavy industry was not entirely in one direction – from Britain to the United States. After 1851 the Singer Sewing Machine Company set up subsidiary factories in Scotland at Govan and Glasgow (1868), shown in the insets (top left and centre). The engraving (right) showing the blast-furnaces of Pittsburgh, Pa, at night, published in *Harper's Weekly* in 1885, evokes the atmosphere of this industrial city which grew up as a centre of iron and steel production.

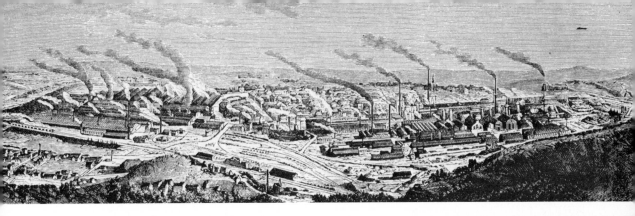

187, 188 In continental Europe two of the principal
centres for the iron and steel industry – both of which
were important in the manufacture of heavy
armaments – were the Schneider Works at Le Creusot
(top) and the Krupp Works at Essen, which by 1880
had developed from a small family business into a vast
complex of steelworks.

189–192 'Invisible exports' from industrialized countries included the technology and expertise necessary for large civil engineering projects in other parts of the world. The excavation of the Suez Canal (above, left) is seen in an engraving published in 1869, and the major engineering works for one of the locks of the Panama Canal (above, right) in a photograph taken in the early years of the present century. These were the great international arteries.

Bridge-building was another important contribution: below are shown a design for the Hooghly River Bridge (with a central cantilever reminiscent of the Forth Bridge) for the East Indian Railway, and the suspension bridge over the Dnieper at Kiev.

193, 194 The City of New York was
the scene of significant engineering
projects and novel developments. The
construction of the Brooklyn Bridge
took a further twelve years after early
problems had been overcome, and was
completed in 1883 – the engraving
above shows the suspension cables
being placed in position.

The solid rock on which New York
was built provided good foundations
for tall buildings, but created
difficulties in tunnelling for
underground railways. The grid
system of the city favoured other
solutions in the provision of public
transport; here, the Battery Station of
the elevated railway (with a local
horse-drawn tram at ground-level)
shows how a steel superstructure above
an existing roadway could provide
a parallel system for passenger traffic.

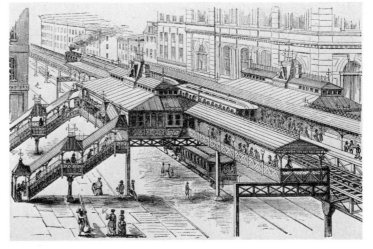

Chronology:
some significant dates

1620 Francis Bacon's *Novum Organum*
1624 Statute of Monopolies regulating patents
1627 Bacon's *New Atlantis*
1655 The Marquess of Worcester's *Century of Inventions*
1660 Foundation of the Royal Society
1663 First Turnpike Act
1681 Completion of the French Canal du Midi
1690 Denis Papin's account of a steam-engine
1694 Foundation of the Bank of England
1698 Thomas Savery's engine 'for raising water by the impellant force of fire'
1701 Jethro Tull's seed-drill
1702 Savery's *The Miner's Friend*: the first practical steam-pump
1709 Abraham Darby I smelts iron with coke
1711 Savery and Thomas Newcomen become partners
1712 A Newcomen engine in use at the colliery at Dudley Castle
1715 Liverpool Old Dock
1716 The Corps des Ingénieurs des Ponts et Chaussées founded in France
1724 Daniel Defoe's *A Tour through Great Britain*
     Thomas Lombe's silk-mill at Derby
1725 The Beckley Burn Embankment
1727 The Causey Arch
1733 John Kay's flying shuttle
     The Fire Engine Act
1734 Birth of Joseph Wright of Derby
1741 Lewis Paul's cotton-mill at Birmingham
1745 E. Lee's windmill fantail patent
1746 John Roebuck manufactures sulphuric acid
1747 The French College of Highways and Bridges founded

1750 Samuel Whitbread acquires the King's Head Brewery
     Anthony Walker's engraving: *Prior Park*
1751 Benjamin Huntsman produces crucible steel at Sheffield
     John Halker's factory at Rouen
1753 First export of a Newcomen engine to Austria
1754 The Society for the Encouragement of Arts, Manufactures and Commerce founded
     John Dalton's *The Mines near Whitehaven*
1755 The Sankey Navigation
1757 John Dyer's *The Fleece*
1758 The 6-mile Middleton railway track near Leeds
1759 Josiah Wedgwood opens his pottery at Burslem
     John Smeaton's Eddystone Lighthouse
     The Dowlais Company
1760 The Carron Iron Works, Glasgow
1761 James Brindley completes the first phase of the Manchester–Worsley Canal
     The first industrial exhibition
1762 Matthew Boulton builds his Soho Manufactory
     John Wilkinson opens ironworks at Broseley, Shropshire
1764 Robert Peel opens a calico-printing business at Blackburn
1765 James Watt's condenser (patented 1769)
     Anthony Bacon leases coal and iron rights at Merthyr Tydfil
1766 The Lunar Society founded in Birmingham
     The Grand Trunk Canal
1767 Francis Moore's 'fire engine for ploughing'
1768 Foundation of the Royal Academy
1769 Richard Arkwright's water-frame

     Jedediah Strutt's ribbed hosiery patent
     Arkwright and Strutt partnership
     Wedgwood opens his Etruria Works
1770 James Hargreaves's patent for the spinning-jenny
     Jesse Ramsden's screw-cutting lathe
1771 Arkwright opens Cromford Mill
     Smeaton founds his Society of Civil Engineers
1772 Andrew Meikle's spring-sail windmill patent
1773 The Turnpike Act
     Birth of Charles Turner
1774 Matthew Boulton and James Watt begin partnership
     Wilkinson's boring-mill patent
1775 The Boulton/Watt steam-engine patent extended for twenty-five years
1776 American Declaration of Independence
     Adam Smith's *Wealth of Nations*
     The Farmer's Magazine
     Glass industry at St Helen's
1779 The first Iron Bridge completed
     Samuel Crompton's 'mule'
1780 James Keir's alkali works at Tipton
1781 Watt's rotative steam-engine
1782 James Cooke's drill
1783 End of the American War of Independence
     Henry Bell's copper cylinder for calico-printing
1784 Henry Cort's puddling process
     Opening of the New Lanark Mill
     Joseph Bramah's lock patent
1785 First steam-driven cotton-mill at Popplewick
     Anna Seward's *Colebrook Dale*
     C. L. Berthollet uses chlorine in bleaching
     Andrew Meikle's threshing-machine

1787 Edmund Cartwright's power-loom patent
Nicolas Leblanc's soda-making process
John Wilkinson's iron barge
Thomas Mead's windmill patent
Watt's governor

1788 Completion of the Albion Mills at Blackfriars
Founding of *The Times*
John Marshall's first water-powered mill at Leeds

1789 The French Revolution begins
Birth of John Martin

1790 First steam-operated rolling-mill in England

1791 The Ordnance Survey established
Completion of Erasmus Darwin's *The Botanic Garden*

1792 Cable-making machine introduced
John Phillips's *General History of Inland Navigation*

1793 Eli Whitney's cotton-gin
War between England and France
Strutt's fire-resistant factory at Milford
The French College of Mines founded

1794 James Cooke's chaff-cutter
The École des Travaux Publiques renamed the École Polytechnique

1795 Bramah's hydraulic press
James Parker's 'Roman cement'

1797 Henry Maudslay's carriage lathe

1798 N.L. Roberts's paper-making machine
William Murdoch produces gas from coal
Thomas Malthus's *Essay on the Principle of Population*

1799 The Royal Institution founded
The Combination Act passed in Britain

1800 The second Combination Act passed
Robert Owen's model factory at New Lanark
Maudslay's precision screw-cutting lathe
The Earl of Stanhope's printing-press
Richard Trevithick's low-pressure steam-engine
Alessandro Volta produces electricity from a cell
Eli Whitney makes muskets with exchangeable parts
Joseph Boyce's reaping-machine
Charles Tennant's lime works

1801 Robert Fulton constructs the first submarine, the *Nautilus*, at Brest
The first English Census
Fireproof cotton-mill at Salford
General Enclosure Act

1802 Du Pont's armaments factory at Wilmington, Del.
Trevithick's successful locomotive trials

1803 Robert Fulton propels a boat by steam-power
The Caledonian Canal begun

1804 James Ryan's coal-boring invention

1805 Completion of the Grand Junction Canal
The Society of Millwrights founded

1806 Nail-cutting machine introduced

1807 The *Clermont* begins a regular steamship service between New York City and Albany

1809 John Heathcoat's lace-making machine
Pall Mall lit by gas

1810 Maudslay's Lambeth Works
The Krupp Works opened at Essen
The Prussian Technical Commission
Trevithick's 'Cornish Engine'

1812 Luddite riots
Henry Bell's daily steamship service on the Clyde
The Gas, Light and Coke Company founded
Philippe Girard's machine for spinning flax

1813 Robert Owen's *New View of Society*
William Hedley's locomotive

1814 *The Times* printed by a steam-powered press
Smooth railway track at Wylam Colliery
George Stephenson's locomotive *Blücher*
Abolition of income tax in Britain

1815 Napoleon defeated at Waterloo
The Corn Law passed
Humphry Davy's safety-lamp
William Smith's geological map of England and Wales

1816 Richard Roberts's machine-tool works at Manchester: screw-cutting lathe
Woolf's compound engine

1817 Joseph Clements's machine-tool works, London
The Institute of Civil Engineers founded

1819 The first Factory Act
The *Savannah* crosses the Atlantic

1820 The Prussian Association for the Promotion of Technical Knowledge
J.L. Macadam's *Present State of Roadmaking*

1821 George Stephenson appointed Engineer to the Stockton and Darlington Railway
The Berlin Technical Institute
The first iron steamship, the *Aaron Manby*
Michael Faraday discovers electromagnetic rotation

1822 Completion of the Caledonian Canal

1823 Charles Babbage begins building his mechanical computer
Roberts's power loom
The first Mechanics' Institute

1824 Portland cement
N.L.S. Carnot's theory of the heat engine
Repeal of the Combination Acts of 1799 and 1800

1825 Opening of the Stockton and Darlington Railway

1826 Patrick Bell's reaping-machine
Telford's Menai Suspension Bridge completed

1827 Joseph Russel's ship's screw
Jacob Perkins's American high-pressure engine
Master weavers' union in Lyons

1828 James Neilson's use of the hot-blast technique at the Clyde Ironworks
The National Union of Cotton Spinners founded

1829 The Rainhill speed trials: victory of Stephenson's *Rocket*

A Bibliographical Note

There is an enormous literature of the 'industrial revolution' and it increases with each year that passes. This highly selective note does not claim to be more than a brief guide, nor does it refer to every book cited in the text. T.S. Ashton's *The Industrial Revolution* (1948) remains the best brief study for the general reader. Phyllis Deane's *The First Industrial Revolution* (1965) takes a longer period into the reckoning, and D.S. Landes's fascinating book *The Unbound Prometheus* (1969) takes in the comparative experience of different countries. So, too, does E.J. Hobsbawm in his brilliant general histories, *The Age of Revolution* (1962) and *The Age of Capital* (1975). R.M. Hartwell, *The Industrial Revolution and Economic Growth* (1971), provides a good background for the historiography of the subject, still in transition, and R.M. Reeves's *The Industrial Revolution*, published in the same year (with the student in mind), was enterprising in including a section on 'looking at the industrial revolution', including 'four faces' – transport, power, workplace and homes.

The historiography of 'looking at' the survivals of the industrial revolution is as interesting as the historiography of 'thinking about' it. F.D. Klingender's *Art and the Industrial Revolution* (1947) was seminal and its bibliography is invaluable, and Anthony Burton's *Remains of a Revolution* (1975) is interesting and beautifully illustrated. Like Reeves, the latter has a useful working bibliography, although it does not give all the dates of publication. Kenneth Hudson's *Industrial Archaeology* (1963) was the admirable first in a line, but see also R.A. Buchanan, *Industrial Archaeology in Great Britain* (1972), and N. Cossons, *The BP Book of Industrial Archaeology* (1975). A series edited by R.R. Green, *The Industrial Archaeology of Great Britain*, provides regional studies, and the Longmans Industrial Archaeology Series, edited by L.T.C. Rolt, provides studies of specific industries.

L.T.C. Rolt's general contribution to the subject-matter of this volume has been enormous, and the best introduction to his many biographies is his own autobiography, *Landscape into Machines* (1971). A worthy predecessor – with a different approach – was H.W. Dickinson; see, for example, his *Matthew Boulton* (1937) or *A Short History of the Steam Engine* (1938). In terms of technical history, much of interest is to be found in the pages of the *Transactions of the Newcomen Society* and (since 1976) of the *Industrial Archaeology Review*.

For buildings and objects, see also J.M. Richards, *The Functional Tradition* (1958), with photographs by Eric de Maré; and local studies like J. Tann, *Gloucestershire Woollen Mills* (1967) and *The Development of the Factory* (1971); G.W. and F.A. Read, *Staffordshire Pots and Potteries* (1906); B. Hillier, *Pottery and Porcelain, 1700–1914* (1968); and *Buildings of Liverpool* (Liverpool Heritage Bureau, 1978). There are many well-planned industrial town trails, just as there are many excellent specialized museums; and W. English gives a good list of those of the latter which specialize in textiles in a gazetteer appended to his *The Textile Industry* (1969).

For social history, which helps to explain much of the visual, J.L. and B. Hammond, *The Rise of Modern Industry* (1925), should be compared with H. Perkin, *The Origins of Modern English Society* (1969), and E.P. Thompson, *The Making of the English Working Class* (1963). W. Bowden, *Industrial Society in England towards the End of the Eighteenth Century* (New York, 1925), although by no means recent, is still not obsolete, however, and S.G. Checkland, *The Rise of an Industrial Society in England* (1964), is more than a textbook.

See also D. Blythell, *The Handloom Weavers* (1969); M.I. Thomis, *The Town Labourer and the Industrial Revolution* (1975); T. Coleman, *The Railway Navvies* (1965); A. Burton, *The Canal Builders* (1972); R. Challinor and B. Ripley, *The Miners' Association* (1968); J.B. Jefferys, *The Story of the Engineers* (1945); and E. Royston Pike, *The Human Documents of the Industrial Revolution* (1966).

The boom in local history, even more than the boom in labour history, has encouraged analysis as much as description, and there are recent books which pass beyond exploration to speculation, like John Money, *Experience and Identity, Birmingham and the West Midlands, 1760–1800* (1977). These may be set alongside older studies like A.H. Dodd, *The Industrial Revolution in North Wales* (1933); and A.H. John, *The Industrial Development of South Wales* (1950). It is necessary, however, to go still further back to the classics like W. Hutton's *A History of Birmingham* (1781); G.R. Porter, *The Progress of the Nation* (1847); Edward Baines, *The History of the Cotton Manufacture in Great Britain* (1835); J. James, *The History of the Worsted Manufacture in England* (1857); W. Fairbairn, *Iron, its*

History, Properties and Processes of Manufacture (1861); F.B. Head, *Stokers and Pokers* (1849); and Arnold Toynbee, *Lectures on the Industrial Revolution in England* (1884).

I used this range of works in my *Victorian Cities* (1963), and among other 'classics' to read are Charles Babbage, *The Economy of Manufactures* (1833); W. Cooke Taylor, *Notes of a Tour in the Manufacturing Districts of Lancashire* (1842); F. Engels, *The Condition of the Working Classes in Manchester* (1958 ed.), and S. Smiles, *Lives of the Engineers* (1861–2). 'Classics' of a more recent date include H. Heaton, *the Yorkshire Woollen and Worsted Industry* (1920), and almost all the works of C.R. Fay.

There are some excellent detailed studies by economic historians. They often cite vivid documentary evidence. Among the most useful are F. Collier, *The Family Economy of the Working Classes in the Cotton Industry, 1784–1833* (1965); G. Unwin (pioneer of social and economic history), *Samuel Oldknow and the Arkwrights* (1924); R.S. Fitton and A.P. Wadsworth, *The Strutts and the Arkwrights* (1958); T.S. Ashton, *Iron and Steel in the Industrial Revolution* (1924); T.S. Ashton and J. Sykes, *The Coal Industry of the Eighteenth Century* (1929); E. Robinson and A.E. Musson, *James Watt and the Steam Revolution* (1969); M.W. Flinn, *Men of Iron* (1962); and W.S. Rimmer, *Marshall's of Leeds* (1960).

Supplementary studies, sometimes reflecting a different range of preoccupations, include S. Lilley, *Men, Machines and History* (1948), a book which would have appealed to Klingender; L. Mumford, *Technics and Cilvilization* (1934); A.P. Usher, *A History of Mechanical Inventions* (1929); T.K. Derry and T.I. Williams, *The Shorter Oxford History of Technology* (1960); W.H.G. Armytage, *A Social History of Engineering* (1961); W.H. Chaloner and A.E. Musson, *Science and Technology* (1967); A.E. Musson and E.R. Robinson, *Science and Technology in the Industrial Revolution* (1969); A. and N. Clew, *The Chemical Revolution* (1952); H.J. Habakkuk, *American and British Technology in the Nineteenth Century* (1962); and K. Luckhurst, *The Story of Exhibitions* (1951).

For railways, see the bibliography in B. Morgan's volume on railways in the Longmans Industrial Archaeology Series (1971); J. Simmons, *The Railways of Britain* (2nd ed., 1968); and M. Robbins, *The Railway Age* (1962). For the visual approach, see M.J.T. Lewis, *Early Wooden Railways* (1970); C. Barman, *An Introduction to Railway Architecture* (1950); and C.V.L. Meek, *The Railway Station* (1957).

J. Warburg has meticulously edited an anthology of illuminating poetry – *The Industrial Muse* (1958) – which should be supplemented by M. Vicinus's book with the same title (1974). F.P. Donavan's *The Railroad in Literature: A Strict Survey* (Boston, Mass., 1940) is still useful, and E.M. Grant's *French Poetry and Modern Industry, 1830–1870* was written as long ago as 1927. L. Marx, *The Machine in the Garden* (1964) is a stimulating essay on technology and the pastoral ideal in the United States.

Finally, for Coalbrookdale and Ironbridge, see A. Raistrick, *Dynasty of Iron Founders: the Darbys . . .* (1953); B. Trinder, *The Industrial Revolution in Shropshire* (1973), and '*The Most Extraordinary District in the World': Ironbridge and Coalbrookdale* (1977); and N. Cossons, *Ironbridge, Landscape of Industry* (1977) with photographs by Harry Sowden.

Index